FALSTAFF AND EQUITY

An Interpretation

BY

CHARLES E. PHELPS

AUTHOR, "JURIDICAL EQUITY;" LAW PROFESSOR,
UNIVERSITY OF MARYLAND; JUDGE,
SUPREME BENCH, BALTIMORE

Falstaff: . . . "An the Prince and Poins be not two arrant cowards, there's no *equity* stirring."

1 Henry IV., Act II. Scene 2.

BOSTON AND NEW YORK
HOUGHTON, MIFFLIN AND COMPANY
The Riverside Press, Cambridge
1902

"I have much to say in the behalf of that Falstaff."

1 Henry IV. Act II. Scene 4.

". . . the purpose of playing . . . to hold, as 't were, the mirror up to nature; to show . . . the very age and body of the time, his form and pressure." *Hamlet, Act III. Scene 2.*

"A jest's prosperity lies in the ear of him that hears it, never in the tongue of him that makes it."

Love's Labour 's Lost, Act V. Scene 2.

"On sait bien que les comédies ne sont faites que pour être jouées, et je ne conseille de lire celle-ci qu' aux personnes qui ont des yeux pour découvrir, dans la lecture, tout le jeu du théâtre." *Molière, L'Amour Médecin, Au Lecteur.*

". . . wherein fat Falstaff
Hath a great scene: the image of the jest
I 'll show you here at large."

Merry Wives of Windsor, Act IV. Scene 6.

PREFACE

With the exception of the short digression on Shakespeare's "School of Insanity" (chapter xiv.), not heretofore published, this commentary is substantially a reproduction of a series of articles contributed to "Shakespeariana," N. Y., in 1892 and 1893, and of a course of lectures at the Peabody Institute, Baltimore, in 1894.

Several years since, the writer challenged the London Notes and Queries, its correspondents and readers, to produce a single reference in print, by way of explanation or comment, to Falstaff's much neglected expression, "There 's no equity stirring."

No answer to the challenge ever appeared in the columns of that journal; but in due time there came a letter from its Shakespearian specialist admitting that no such allusion was anywhere to be found. The writer then forwarded to his English correspondent, Mr. Sam Timmins, F. S. A. (the well-known "Este" of the N. & Q., a Life Trustee of the Shakespeare Birthplace, and one of the Governors and Council of the Shakespeare Memorial), the closing number of the series, summing up the results of the investigation, to which "Este" or S. T. was good enough to reply, and the writer is now modest enough to quote: "Your paper is original. You seem to have the field to yourself, and you have scored many good points."

Special acknowledgments are due to Dr. Horace Howard Furness of Philadelphia, author of the New Variorum edition; to Appleton Morgan, Esq., President of the New York Shakespeare Society; to Prof. John Ordronaux of New York; to the cherished memory of the late Richard Malcolm Johnston of Baltimore, and to Henry Austin Clapp, Esq., of Boston (who is only mentioned last because he is here to speak for himself) for their early and appreciative recognition of the leading idea of this commentary, when presented in its first and tentative form. To Richard Savage, Esq., Librarian at the Shakespeare Birthplace, and to W. Salt Brassington, F. S. A., Librarian of the Shakespeare Memorial, and to their assistants, the writer is indebted for courteous attentions in the inspection of records at Stratford-on-Avon.

The conclusions of the investigation herein traced are all drawn from authentic record evidence, and from actual reported cases, both civil and criminal. These old records and cases, and the new lessons they teach, when placed in natural relations with each other and with Falstaff, will be found of especial interest to all English-speaking judges, lawyers, and law-students, to all students of the Elizabethan era, and to all interested in Shakespeare's personal biography.

There will be found in *Appendix A* a chronology of the "war between the courts" from the first collision between the laws of England and Rome in the twelfth century down to the final triumph of equity in sixteen hundred and sixteen.

There will be found collected in *Appendix B* the original documents of the cases of Shakespeare *v.* Lambert in the court of common pleas, in the court of queen's bench, and in the high court of chancery. *Appendix C*, "Shakespeare a Party to the Lambert Compromise," will be found "caviare to the general," and will be judiciously skipped by all but the elect.

The references to the Outlines of the Life of Shakespeare by J. O. Halliwell-Phillips are to the *ninth edition*, except where otherwise noted.

C. E. P.

BALTIMORE, February, 1901.

CONTENTS

INTRODUCTION

I HAVE yielded to Judge Phelps's flattering wish that I should write an introduction to his essay on "Falstaff and Equity," warning him that he has no need of me, and that from my compliance with his request may flow the obvious inconvenience that it may be necessary for him to procure somebody to introduce his introducer. Of all the good wines of authorship, surely the most bushless in need is that which is expressed in sound criticism of the Master Poet. As long as the English language is spoken, — as long, even, as it is read, — the judicious few, whose censure must outweigh a world's stageful of others, will hail with joy and gratitude the work of the man who can throw so much as the narrowest pencil of light upon any obscure word or phrase of Shakespeare.

The discovery, made by the essayist and committed to the print of this volume, seems to me to be of its kind the most curious, interesting, and surprising candle of illumination that has been newly lighted within several years. The text of the great Falstaff had been submitted to the threshing of three centuries; and, during that time, no editor, commentator, or critic had found any matter for comment in Sir John's familiar outburst of peevish delight after the robbing of the travelers, "An the Prince and Poins be not two arrant cowards, there's no *equity stirring*." Only Mr. Ignatius Donnelly, poking the fat ribs of the knight in search for bacon, brought his mind to bear upon the passage and delivered himself of the opinion that the clause "there's no equity stirring" is "forced and unnatural." And now comes an American judge and law-professor, and, despite his distance from Stratford and the English courts, compels the ancient records to give up the facts which translate the dramatist's line out of commonplace into vivacious and effective wit. Perhaps it will please Sir John, if he can look up from where he is, — or look down from where he is, if his devoted hostess's opinion of his locus is correct, — to see that that brain of his, — ever "apprehensive, quick, forgetive, full of nimble, fiery, and delectable shapes," even without the stimulating and vapor-drying effects of sherries-sack, has been justified at last.

In the last two sentences is indicated my only difference of opinion with Judge Phelps in his discussion. I am convinced that the value of his discovery would be much enhanced if he discarded altogether the idea that "equity" in the passage dealt with has, even for the least important of its meanings, "justice" in the common use of that word. Falstaff's proposition is this: That the Prince and Poins are two arrant cowards is certain, as certain as anything can be that is most certain. Then what is his standard of certainty? The abundance or stir of "justice" in the world? Could any comparison be weaker, or more distinctively un-Falstaffian? Sir John often cynically proclaimed that there was no such thing as justice anywhere on earth. It is not as if he were saying, if the Prince and Poins are not *punished* for their cowardice, there's no justice in this world,—a remark which might pass as unimportant. If Falstaff's shout, at the topmost point of the exciting situation, is to be paraphrased thus, *That the Prince and Poins are two arrant cowards is as certain as that justice abounds,* then Sir John is to be convicted, for the first, last, and only time in his career, of saying something flat and unprofitable at a critical moment. That is, to my mind, an irresistible argument against any toleration of the paraphrase which everybody had accepted as an equivalent of the clause until our essayist brought the search-light of his learning to bear upon the text of Shakespeare and the context of legal history.

The learning of the essay, so careful, exact, and opulent; the reasoning of the essay, so lucid, valid, and convincing—received with joy by the readers of "Shakespeariana" and now offered to a larger circle — attempt, after all, to do little more than inform a modern audience with what was the common knowledge of the crowd in an Elizabethan theatre. But Judge Phelps has had the happy experience which has often come to the honest and industrious investigator, — of seeing his work grow under his hands, of finding that what at first seemed like a mere "pocket" of gold has proved to be a genuine "fissure vein." All his readers, whether of his own profession or otherwise, will be delighted with his explication of the long historic struggle in England between the courts of common law and chancery. And what honest Shakespearean can refrain from pleasant excitement at the demonstration that, within the ten years between 1588 and 1598, the warfare of the two faces of the Janus-head of the English judiciary had reached a point of extreme acuteness? Under Judge Phelps's treatment, the *cause célèbre* of the variously orthographied "ambidexter" defendant, Heal, Heale, Hele, Heele, Heyle, or Hale; the equally noted suit in equity of Throckmorton *v.* Finch; the extraordinary process of Mylward *v.* Weldon, and the now illustrious bill in equity of Shakespeare *v.* Lambert, from which the dramatist probably got one course of lessons in "the law's delay," — all these are compelled to "smell sweet and blossom in the dust" superimposed upon them by three hundred years. It is shown that the air of London had quivered with the excitement of the contest between the "robed man of justice" and his "yoke fellow of equity," and that the name of the writ "premunire" — about the extremely learned allusion to which, in Henry VIII., the Baconians have made such a vain fuss — might have been in the mouths of fishmongers and drapers. When, finally, it is shown "of record" that the famous order punishing the scrivener in Mylward *v.* Weldon for "the inordinate length and prolixity of his replication" was entered February 10, 1596–7; that the decision of the twelve judges of England against the chancellor, in Throckmorton *v.* Finch, was made November 15, 1597; that, nine days later, to wit, on the 24th of November, 1597, John and Mary Shakespeare filed a new bill in equity in Shakespeare *v.* Lambert for the possession of the Arden family estate of Asbies; and when this record testimony is collated with the received opinion that the First Part of Henry IV. was produced, either early in 1597, or about the Christmas holidays of that year; — the contemporary "stirring" of "equity" and the value of the illustration for purposes of immediate popular effect are splendidly demonstrated. Falstaff is made to win again as always, with the laugh from gentle and simple approving the admirable dexterity of his wit.

The unfailing charm, freshness, and vitality of the essayist's style will be sufficiently appreciated without any hints or helps from the introducer.

HENRY AUSTIN CLAPP.

BOSTON, December, 1900.

FALSTAFF AND EQUITY

CHAPTER I

FALSTAFF AT GADSHILL

Falstaff's "no equity stirring" the climax of the Gadshill incident. — A jest that requires explanation. — No light from the commentators. — A local hit, or gag.

GENTLE readers ought in all fairness to be warned, at the outset, that they will be expected to submit, without the comfort of chloroform, to the most excruciating operation known to literary surgery, *the explanation of a joke.*

They may also be flattered with the hope that the explanation may carry with it some instructive insight into the environment of Falstaff, which means the environment of Falstaff's creator; may unearth some forgotten quarrel which alternately excited the anger and the mirth of the age of Elizabeth, and may shed some new side-light upon the scantily known private life of the world's greatest dramatic poet.

The proceeding first in order is, of course, the announcement of the subject-matter.

It is a serious thing to undertake to announce something as a joke that does not go of itself. The reaction is always depressing. It makes one feel thoughtful. The effect may be compared to that at a festive reunion when, amid "the feast of reason and the flow of soul," all levity is hushed as there falls upon the ear, with solemn cadence, that sobering toast, "To the Judiciary."

The modern mind will find it difficult to realize that words from which the volatile spirit has so completely evaporated that little more is left of them than an empty sound, of so little apparent significance that they have been on all hands contemptuously ignored, actually conveyed to a London audience of the sixteenth century a vivid association of familiar ideas, which in their day made the allusion both exciting and ludicrous — worthy in fact of "the most humorous figure in literature" [1] at the very climax of his most telling situation.

The expression occurs in the short speech which accentuates and, so far as words are concerned, practically closes the Gadshill incident, — the incident of all Falstaff's situations the most famous and popular. There is but one

[1] Sidney Lee's Life of Shakespeare, p. 171. "A kind of English Bacchus." "A creature of the elemental forces." "A satyr become human, moving buoyantly and joyfully in an unmoral world." (William Shakespeare, Poet, Dramatist, and Man, by H. W. Mabie.)

possible competitor for public favor, and that is the buck-basket scene.[1] The capital point in which the Gadshill adventure distances all rivals for applause is in the actual presence upon the stage of a live prince and heir-apparent.

It will be recalled how Prince Hal and Poins, carrying out their waggish understanding at Falstaff's expense, have merrily contrived to absent themselves at the critical moment, thus leaving Sir John with the interesting Bardolph and the rest to rob the travelers without their aid. At the point of time which intervenes between two actions of great heat and violence performed upon the stage, — first, the highway robbery, and then the sudden attack by the Prince and Poins upon Falstaff and his crowd, and the ignominious surrender of their booty, — a very short sub-scene is interposed. What little is said is said by the fat knight himself, and the whole performance is as follows: —

> "Reënter thieves. *Fals.* Come, my masters, let us share and then to horse before day. An the Prince and Poins be not two arrant cowards, *there 's no equity stirring.* There 's no more valor in that Poins than in a wild duck." [2]

To modern readers, not coached, this short scene is anything but a brilliant success. They fail to be at all impressed by the singular allusion to "no equity stirring." They can find in the

[1] *Merry Wives of Windsor*, Act III. scene 3.

[2] *1 Henry IV.* Act. II. scene 2.

words nothing to warrant their interjection in the mouth of such a character, at the crowning height of such a situation.

Falstaff has to sustain, upon every occasion, that most oppressive of all reputations, the character of a professional jester. He is nothing if not funny. When he ceases to amuse, we have no further use for him: he, "that old, white-bearded Satan," is simply an "advanced omelette" without salt. Even when at the end of his jokes and of his life, we must have the unconscious humor of Dame Quickly — who, "to comfort him, bid him a' should not think of God" — to lighten, with a flash of mirth, the pathos of the jester's deathbed scene.[1]

Here, he has the great opportunity of his life. Has he not just shown himself a thief, and is he not about showing himself a coward? Nay, as to this very transaction, is he not a little later on to show himself a mammoth liar? Now, for one supreme moment he has the stage to himself. All eyes are centred upon his greasy personality, and expectation is on tiptoe to hear the hoary fraud and braggart redeem himself, at least, as a wag.

Instead of that, he gives us — what? A phrase apparently so pointless, tame, flat, and feeble, that the commentators all turn from it with averted faces; that in a popular so-called "Life of Falstaff" it is actually suppressed, as

[1] *Henry V.* Act II. scene 3.

not worth quoting;[1] and that the only critic who has ever condescended to notice it at all spurns at it and kicks it aside.[2]

Such was the sorry plight in which the passage was found, a very "Cinderella of literature,"[3] when, as an incidental side-show to another subject of inquiry, an investigation happened to be started from the contemporaneous point of view of the struggle over the jurisdiction of equity between the court of chancery and the courts of common law.

Upon this line, some startling coincidences of dates were discovered, and a number of surprising revelations turned up. The despised empty phrase was found loaded to the muzzle with contemporaneous, local meaning, rich, varied, and vivid. No happy or unhappy "conjectural emendation" was required. Nothing wanted to be read into the text, or read out of it. All that was needed was simply to take the text exactly as Shakespeare made it, not attempting to translate it into any supposed equivalent. All difficulty vanished the moment the words were understood as Falstaff was supposed to understand them, and as Falstaff's audience did actually understand them.

[1] Brough's Life of Falstaff, illustrated by Cruikshank, London, Longmans, 1858.

[2] "The language here is forced; this is not a natural expression." (Hon. Ignatius Donnelly, Great Cryptogram, 524.)

[3] A term applied by some one (Malone?) to the Sonnets.

Exactly what that understanding was, it is the purpose of these pages to develop in detail.

It will be shown, upon record evidence of the highest authenticity, that, at the precise juncture, such a state of circumstances notoriously existed as made Falstaff's fling, when he had the stage to himself, what would now be called an effective and brilliant "play to the galleries." It was one of those sudden turns or tricks, unexpected, sensational, showy, ludicrously incongruous with the situation, while artfully appealing to a present and passionate outside interest, comically yoked with an irresistibly droll association, that, for want of a better English word, we have to call *coups de théâtre*. A better English word is at hand, if slang were in order. It was a "gag." And a more timely gag was never devised, nor a more telling one. It was in fact, as well as in time and in place, the crown of the Gadshill incident.

That was when it was alive. Now that it is dead, buried, forgotten and dug up, the poor old thing lies upon the table, a mere anatomical specimen, awaiting dissection. We are three hundred years behind Falstaff, but a good many more than three hundred ideas ahead of him. It will take considerably less than that number of minutes to "catch on to his curves," although "I have much to say in the behalf of that Falstaff." [1]

[1] *1 Henry IV.* Act II. scene 4.

CHAPTER II

"EQUITY" IN LITERATURE

Its uniform Bible use. — Its various uses in Shakespeare. — Its use by Falstaff.

"THERE is something very curious," says Halliwell-Phillips, speaking of Shakespearian commentators, "in the way in which early facts of critical importance are being continually overlooked, although they may be almost before our eyes in common or easily accessible books."

On the other hand, it is equally true that minute and microscopic examination or reëxamination of very common objects often leads to curious discoveries. Those who take the time and trouble to make such examinations, while they may sometimes discover mares' nests, and may sometimes have their labor for their pains, will occasionally be fortunate enough to perceive facts, or relations of facts, that had escaped general observation. Unexpected revelations of this nature may come incidentally, quite off the direct line of original inquiry. The naturalist, for instance, who is engaged in close investigation of the fat and sticky little aphis, will encounter surprising developments as to the habits and intelligence of that model business man, the ant. The fundamental principle of the electric motor was incidentally discovered by Oersted while verifying one of Faraday's experiments. Industrial enterprises of various kinds incidentally furnish by-products which often compare in value with that of the main object of manufacture. And so it is with what may be called the by-products of investigation. There are many things well worth knowing that are never learned except in a laborious and persevering effort to learn something else.

Several years since, it happened to the writer, for a special purpose, to make as thorough research as he was capable of making into the historical origin of equity jurisprudence. The purpose was the preparation of lectures for an advanced class of law students. One of the lines upon which the investigation was pursued was found to lead into the track of a familiar but neglected passage of Shakespeare, the full meaning of which had never been explored. And it came about in this way. The effort was to determine from original sources, quite independently of text-books and of what is commonly called "authority," the exact place and value in English literature of the word "equity" itself.[1] Naturally

[1] It is not, of course, suggested that no such investigation had ever been made before. It is sufficient to say that no trace

rally, the first resort was to the English Bible and Shakespeare.

In the New Testament the word does not occur. In the Old Testament Scriptures the word rendered in the standard English version "equity" is found in close connection with such terms as "righteousness," "justice," "judgment," "wisdom," "truth," and in contrast with "iniquity."[1]

Sometimes the same word is rendered in one version "equity" and in another "uprightness"[2] or "justice."[3] Collation of texts exhibits "equity" in the Bible use as a complex ethical conception, covering that department of morals which inculcates absolute good faith; involving the idea of integrity and impartiality, equality of right in theory and fairness in practice. Briefly, it stands for *justice* in the broad sense of the Roman law, *jus suum cuique tribuere*, *jus* being used in opposition to *lex*. But the principal point to be noted here is, that in the Bible the word "equity" *is invariably used in the same general sense.*

With regard to the use of the term by Shakespeare, the case is notably and altogether different. In the whole of Shakespeare's works, the

of any such inquiry was anywhere to be found, productive of the results herein developed.

[1] Ps. 98: 9; 99: 4. Prov. 1: 13; 2: 9; 17: 26. Ecc. 2: 21. Isa. 11: 4; 59: 14. Mic. 3: 9. Mal. 2: 6.

[2] Ps. 111: 8. [3] Ps. 89: 14.

word occurs but four times, and *each time with distinctly varied import.* The following arrangement of the four passages is entirely arbitrary and for present convenience: —

> "Foul subornation is predominant,
> And equity exiled your highness' land."
> (*2 Henry VI.* Act III. scene 1.)

> "Thou robed man of justice, take thy place,
> And thou, his yoke-fellow of equity,
> Bench by his side."
> (*Lear*, Act III. scene 6.)

> "For this down-trodden equity we tread
> In warlike march these greens before your town."
> (*K. John*, Act II. scene 1.)

The fourth passage is the one in question: —

> "There 's no equity stirring."
> (*1 Henry IV.* Act II. scene 2.)

Upon closely comparing these passages, it became quite manifest that in each of the first three the word is used in a different sense. For instance, in *2 Henry VI.* equity is used in the Bible sense, as roughly synonymous with justice.[1] In *Lear*, it is connected with, but sharply distinct from, justice, and the reference is to juridical or technical equity,[2] the equity of the appro-

[1] Compare especially Isa. 59 : 14, "And judgment is turned away backward, and justice standeth afar off : for truth is fallen in the street, and equity cannot enter."

[2] Furness, Var. Ed., *Lear*, 209. "Lear's conception, in his insane caprice, is that the Fool is a justice of a court of common law, and that Edgar is the chancellor." (Davis's The Law in Shakespeare, 246, second edition.)

priate courts. In *John* it is used in the still more narrow and special sense of a concrete equitable right, or ground for specific equitable relief, a term of art perfectly familiar to lawyers, and here employed of course figuratively.[1]

The question came up, In which of these three senses is the word used by Falstaff? An investigation followed which resulted in a series of surprises. By successive stages the discovery was reached, whether real or imaginary it must be for the candid reader to determine, that in the expression of Falstaff, "*There's no equity stirring*," the word equity is used *in all three of the above-mentioned senses at once.* It is used, first, in the Bible sense of justice; second, in the juridical sense of the equity of the court of chancery, and in this sense with a twofold application; and third, in the professional sense of an equitable cause of action. In other words, we strike here one of those pregnant phrases surcharged not with a double or triple but with quadruplex meaning, in which the subtle genius of the poet delighted to revel. He has one meaning for posterity and for all time; two other meanings for his immediate audience, for stage effect, and for contemporaries; and still another meaning for Shakespeare himself, his family, his friends, and his Stratford neighbors. This is a broad claim, and now for the proof.

[1] See the writer's Juridical Equity, sec. 131.

CHAPTER III

JURIDICAL EQUITY

Equity, in the sense of "justice," the heretofore accepted interpretation. — Further explanation in contemporaneous events and characters. — Juridical equity. — Its expanding jurisdiction. — Ellesmere. — Opposition of the judges. — Coke. — The war between the courts. — Criminal prosecutions. — "Stir" caused thereby. — The phrase a localism.

THERE is of course no sort of difficulty with respect to the first assigned signification. So far as I have been able to ascertain, the universal acceptation of "equity" in this passage has been that of *justice*, and there has been no suggestion anywhere of any other.[1] The silence of commentators is profound and unanimous. In none of the numerous editions, old or new, is there the slightest notice taken of this passage. Like the unfrequented offices of the neglected Irish lawyer, they are "swarming with absentees." It seems to have been taken for granted on all

[1] In Dr. Alexander Schmidt's Shakespeare-Lexicon, second edition, 1886, Berlin and London, the word "equity" is defined simply "justice," and the passage in question is one of the four references noted. Absolutely conclusive, so far as that authority goes, that no other meaning had been accepted.

hands that there can be but one meaning attached to the words, and that that meaning is too plain for comment or illustration.

Failing to find anything in print, application was made to living experts, professional Shakespearian scholars and lecturers. The interpretation put upon this passage by each of the experts independently was substantially to the same effect. In form, the phrase is an adjuration, a mild oath. In substance, "no equity stirring" is equivalent to "*no such thing as justice going.*" The point of the joke is that such a character as Falstaff should appeal to such a thing as justice or equity at all, and especially in connection with a transaction so inequitable as a highway robbery.

This interpretation is so perfectly "in line with Falstaff's audacious humor" (to borrow the words of a correspondent[1]) that it is not difficult

[1] Henry Austin Clapp, Esq., who, in the letter referred to, writes: "I should paraphrase the sentence thus: If the Prince and Poins be not two arrant cowards there is no such thing as active or achieving justice in this world, or, there is no justice alive and efficient in this world. Probably the ellipsis suggested is: And we know there is such a thing as justice for just such arrant cowards. The allusion to justice or 'equity' in the transaction is in the line of the audacious humor of Falstaff,— is it not? Another man might hesitate before suggesting that the principle of 'equity' was alive at the moment of completing such a very inequitable proceeding as highway robbery, but Falstaff would relish the antithesis." Comparing this with the critical part of the Introduction (*ante*), it would seem as if, somehow, like Hamlet and Laertes, Mr. Clapp and I had swapped foils. The letter was dated December 14, 1889.

to account for its universal acceptance. It appears to cover the whole ground. *Prima facie* the explanation is so entirely satisfactory and complete that any further inquiry has been deemed superfluous.

But the words, "*there's no justice going*," are not Shakespeare's choice, although it may be thought they would have answered his purpose equally well. The choice of words here is not controlled or perturbed by any metrical exigency. We may safely assume that Shakespeare had his own reasons for his selection in this instance, as in most others. Why should he have preferred the word "equity" here to "justice"? Why should he have chosen such a word as "stirring," a term often suggestive of something more than mere activity or alertness, and in a frequent sense pregnant with the idea of agitation, excitement, intensity?

Whatever opinion may be held on the mooted question of Shakespeare's practical connection, at any time or in any capacity, with the legal profession, one thing at least is certain. No one will deny that he was a wide-awake and all-alive observer of passing events. Beyond all question, he was a well-informed contemporary of Ellesmere, of Coke, and of Bacon. He was an appreciative witness of the great contest between the courts of law and equity, in which those men acted conspicuous parts. He had doubtless heard the merits of the controversy discussed many times in the well-informed circles to which he had access. He very well knew that upon a question so notoriously in evidence as the power of the chancellor to restrain proceedings at law by the process of injunction, especially after judgment, the two sides of Westminster Hall were at swords' points.

Direct confirmation of these statements will be found farther on in the circumstances connected with the case of Shakespeare *v.* Lambert, pending in the court of chancery at the time the drama was in preparation.

Three years before the appearance of Falstaff upon the stage, Sir Thomas Egerton commenced his famous judicial career as master of the rolls, and in two years became Lord Chancellor Ellesmere. He was a resolute and determined character, and fully believed in the maxim that it is "the office of a good judge to amplify his jurisdiction." Lord Campbell styles him the "*earliest founder of our system of equity.*" [1]

[1] Camp. Lives Chan. ch. xlv. In point of fact, Ellesmere was not the "earliest" nor the only "founder of equity," discovered by Campbell. In this connection, the writer begs leave to introduce a relevant paragraph from his Juridical Equity, under the head "Genesis of Equity:" "Research into the origin of institutions, when pressed back to the initial stage whence all development issues, gropes in the twilight of a strange and rudimentary condition, and is sometimes lost in myth. As said by Niebuhr, in his History of Rome (i. 55), 'All absolute beginning lies beyond the reach of our mental conceptions, which com-

"Founders" of systems do not ordinarily contribute to the quiet and repose of their times.

prehend nothing beyond development and progress.' It is so with the origin of that supplementary system of English law called equity jurisprudence or juridical equity. The term 'Equity jurisprudence' is commonly, although not necessarily, used in contradistinction to 'equity procedure.' The broader term 'Juridical equity' includes both.

"For over a thousand years the succession of English chancellors who are responsible for its establishment may be traced back to a legendary saint (A. D. 836, legend of St. Swithin). Three centuries later, the norm of primitive equity is first distinctly disclosed in a rude couplet, which sums up the judicial career of another saint and a martyr, Thomas à Becket.

> Hic est qui leges regni cancellat iniquas
> Et mandata pii principis æqua facit.

"Coming down two centuries more, we are told that the 'foundation of equity' was laid by Parnynge, the first lay-lawyer who held the office of chancellor, A. D. 1343. Again we learn that the same 'foundation' was laid by John de Waltham, A. D. 1386, by his invention of the writ of *subpœna*, when master of the rolls. Still later we are informed that some have ascribed the 'origin of equity jurisdiction' to the chancellorship of Cardinal Beaufort, in the reign of Henry V., while others assign that honor to Cardinal Wolsey in the reign of Henry VIII. (Camp. Lives Chan. ch. i., xiv., xvi., xix., xxviii.) By this time it might be reasonably supposed that the real 'founder' had been found, and we are therefore inclined to be somewhat surprised at the information we are next to receive, that Lord Chancellor Ellesmere, in the reign of Elizabeth, was considered as 'the earliest founder of our system of equity.' (Ibid. ch. xlv.) But that is not all. After reposing upon that assurance for nearly a century, the discovery is yet to be made, that in the reign of Charles II. we at length find the real 'father of equity' in Sir Heneage Finch, Lord Chancellor Nottingham. (Ibid. ch. xci.)

"In all this apparent contradiction and real obscurity, there is no occasion for surprise. The 'absolute beginning' eludes

To found anything of importance involves departure from the established order, and that of course spells opposition, friction, collision, agitation. The opposition to Ellesmere was headed by the twelve judges of England, incited and braced by Sir Edward Coke, then attorney-general. Coke was a rugged, blackletter lawyer, with popular sympathies, jealous of arbitrary power, and, if possible, a more positive and uncompromising character than the chancellor.

It was by no means difficult to excite alarm by pointing to the usurpations and encroachments of the court of chancery. Its "extraordinary jurisdiction" was unsettled; it had no clearly defined limits; much was left to the chancellor's "discretion," and for that discretion there was said to be no standard or measure but the "length of the chancellor's foot." [1]

The most aggressive arm of the chancellor was the injunction. There is no mystery and but little technicality about this process. A mother who forbids her little boy from putting his feet in the gutter lays upon him an injunction; and when the little boy, in contempt of court, disobeys, she gives him, with her slipper, a practical illustration of the jurisdiction *in personam*.

our grasp. The successive stages of growth are all that we discover. Each new departure stands for a new beginning." (Phelps's Juridical Equity, sec. 129.)

[1] Selden, Table Talk, iv. 2028.

That, in the last analysis, is all that an injunction amounts to in substance, — a prohibition or a command, and a penalty for disobedience. So long as the chancellor was content to interfere in this manner to restrain the commission of waste, or nuisance, or destructive trespass, there had never been any complaint more serious than an occasional growl. But the chancellor found it impossible to carry into effect the jurisdiction he had assumed of controlling the rigor of the law by "conscience" without interference with legal proceedings, often intolerably harsh and absurdly unjust.

Injunctions were therefore issued to restrain parties from proceeding with inequitable lawsuits, and at that point equity struck the line of battle of the common law. This was denounced as an unjustifiable interference with the sacred right of Englishmen to obtain injustice by the verdict of a jury. And usurpation disclosed its most offensive form when it laid its hand upon the very palladium, by actually prohibiting the execution of a common law judgment, solemnly recorded upon the verdict of "twelve good and lawful men."

Against such interference, the judges had from the first stoutly protested. They took the extreme ground that they would not respect such injunctions. They encouraged their suitors to defy them. They threatened to release on *habeas corpus* any common law suitor who should be imprisoned by the chancellor for their violation. Defendants, or their counsel, who should apply to the chancellor for such relief, the judges threatened with criminal prosecution. These threats were not vain flourishes, but were actually carried into effect.[1]

The judges felt very strong in their position as against the chancellor for two substantial reasons.

1. They relied upon what they claimed to be the express terms of several acts of parliament.[2]

2. It was exclusively for the courts of law to pronounce, in the last resort, upon the jurisdictional validity of a contested decree, since those courts alone possessed the power of punishing criminally, or of redressing by civil action for damages, cases of homicide or assault in which the execution of a doubtful decree might be resisted by violence.[3]

The chancellor, on the other hand, felt equal

[1] Humphrey's case, Crompton on Courts, 60 ; Heal's case, and several other cases reported by Coke, 3 Inst. 123, 124.

[2] Notably, the statute of "*premunire*," 27 Edward III., so called from the leading word in this writ, a corrupt form of *præmonere*, "to warn," by which the sheriff was charged to summon delinquents, "*which do sue in any other court to defeat or impeach the judgments given in the king's court.*" Also, the statute of "prohibition" (4 Henry IV.) declaring that "*judgments at law should not be annulled excepting by attaint or for error.*"

[3] Forum Romanum, 77; Coleston *v.* Gardner, 2 Ch. Ca. 43; De Lolme, Const. of Eng. i. ch. xi. 151; Phelps's Jurid. Eq. sec. 237.

confidence in the strength of his position, as against the courts of law. It was, always had been, and in fact still is, the accepted maxim at the basis of English jurisprudence, that the crown is the "fountain of justice." [1]

The chancellor stood between the "fountain" and the judges. He had, in fact, the principal hand in their appointment. They exercised in all civil cases a derivative power only, a power derived from certain formulas called "writs," framed and issued under his supervision and control.

By scholastic reasoning and by chop-logic, mediæval judges had dug deep ruts of precedent which so narrowed the scope and application of these formulas or "writs" that the law courts found themselves, or thought they found themselves, helpless to deal out justice in large and constantly growing classes of civil cases. Parliament in vain sought to reform the increasing evil. The salutary purposes of the statute [2] were in great measure defeated by an obstinate judicial conservatism. The courts persisted in failing to redress many cases of palpable injustice.

That meant simply a residuum of judicial power remaining in the king, not as yet delegated to his courts of law, — hence, applications for relief

[1] 1 Bl. Com. 266; 3 Bl. Com. 273; Coomber's case, 9 App. Ca. 67.

[2] Westminster II., 13 Edw. I.

directly to the "fountain," the king in person, naturally referred by him to an appropriate official, who was at once his secretary, the keeper of his seal, the keeper of his "conscience," hence, the "lord keeper" and the constant attendant upon his person.

This powerful official was, of course, the lord chancellor, the most influential personage in the kingdom. His influence was intrenched behind an impregnable breastwork of "patronage," political, judicial, and ecclesiastical. He was the conspicuous type of all successful men — the men who "get there." He was the representative of the party in power — came in with it and went out with it. He was the sovereign's right-hand man. Against the jealousy of parliaments, against the obstructions of the courts of law, in all its struggles to maintain and enlarge its equitable jurisdiction, his court, the high court of chancery, "the court of your absolute power," as Bacon assured James the First, had always relied with implicit confidence upon the steady support of the reigning monarch.[1]

In Elizabeth, last of the Tudors, Ellesmere saw upon the throne the dauntless spirit of her race. Counting upon her unflinching support, he was prepared, in spite of all opposition, to push the jurisdiction of equity to its amplest verge. At the same time, as has been pointed out, the atti-

[1] See Appendix A.

tude of the twelve judges, inspired and encouraged by Sir Edward Coke, the queen's attorney-general, was that of stubborn defiance.

From the reported cases to be cited in their place, it will appear that at the time the drama now in question was in course of preparation, these opposing elements had come into violent collision, thus bringing to an acute stage the quarrel that had been for many years in progress.

The personal acerbity and bitterness which flavored the quarrel Shakespeare may be supposed to have thoroughly appreciated, and the "humor of it." The exciting personal incidents which from time to time punctuated its progress were as familiar to him as to the entire legal profession and the intelligent public. He, in common with all his contemporaries, had taken note of the repeated attempts at criminal prosecution of suitors who had dared to invoke the obnoxious interference of the chancery with proceedings in the courts of law.

A criminal prosecution under a statute denouncing such dreadful penalties upon conviction as imprisonment for life and sweeping confiscation of property was a very serious matter. Such a statute was the statute of *premunire* of 27 Edw. I. It denounced these penalties against all those "which do sue in any other court to defeat or impeach the judgments given in the king's court."[1] This statute had been repeatedly construed by the law courts as including the court of chancery as well as the courts ecclesiastical and foreign. Every suitor who ventured to file an injunction bill for relief against an unconscientious judgment did so with the awful threat of a *premunire* hanging over his head. There had been no actual convictions, but a number of prosecutions for this particular cause, and each of these cases became a new storm centre.

When a person of any importance and of good repute is indicted upon a serious criminal charge there is apt to be a stir throughout the community. The friends and acquaintances of the party are naturally aroused. What has he done? What is going to be done with him? And when the prosecution involves such a charge as that of a *premunire* the wave of inquiry, comment, and agitation spreads rapidly. Lawyers especially, of every grade and of either side of the profession, solicitors in chancery, attorneys at law, barristers, sergeants, all watch developments with intense interest. Whatever stirs the legal profession, if intelligible outside, stirs the entire public. Lawyers will be talking, and they will take sides. Almost to a man the common law bar will be found maintaining, as the judges maintained, that the indictment is good. With equal unanimity the chancery bar and the solicitors

[1] 3 Inst. 119.

will be found on the side of the traverser. The question at issue is not a barren technicality, unintelligible and uninteresting outside the profession. It is not like the controversy over the application of the *rule in Shelley's case* to the facts of the case of Perrin *v.* Blake,[1] which more than a century later resulted in the dismemberment of the court of king's bench. That controversy profoundly stirred the bar,[2] but was too subtle and refined, too exclusively professional, for public interest.

The war between the courts of equity and common law involved issues perfectly plain to the public apprehension and elements of universal interest. In one aspect, it was a simple question between a jury of twelve men and the one-man power of adjudication. In another, it was a question of whether the "corrupt conscience" of a successful litigant should be permitted to retain an inequitable advantage.

Historically, the controversy was in the direct line of descent from the old struggle for jurisdiction between the temporal and ecclesiastical courts, between the common and civil law, between England and Rome. Politically, it connected with the great struggle against the pretensions of the crown to arbitrary power, a power

[1] 4 Burrow, 2579.

[2] It gave birth to that once admired, but now neglected, legal classic, Fearne on Contingent Remainders.

distrusted when exhibited in the chancery almost as much as in the star chamber. And the political aspect linked this judicial controversy with the great religious movement of the age and of former ages.[1]

The Puritan and Presbyterian would naturally side with the judges. The Catholic and High Churchman would as naturally incline to the chancellor.

Thus all parties, all classes, and all creeds in the community were touched upon a sensitive nerve whenever the news spread like wildfire that another indictment had been found against a suitor in chancery. There was intense feeling, much discussion, general excitement and agitation. The agitation, indeed, was so palpable a fact, so notorious and undeniable, that it was fit to pass into a byword. It was a standard fact that might be adjured, attested, appealed to, sworn by. If such and such is not so, "there 's no equity stirring."

The secondary and deeper meaning attributed to this passage now begins to show through the surface. In this sense the words were used "*ad captandum*," for local color and for immediate stage effect. They were so used in line with Hamlet's opinion as to the real "purpose of play-

[1] In ecclesiastical history, the statute of *premunire* furnishes the clue that connects the constitutions of Clarendon with the Reformation. (Stubbs's Const. Hist. xix. 393.)

ing, whose end, both at the first and now, was, and is, to hold, as 't were, the mirror up to Nature; to show Virtue her own feature, Scorn her own image, and the very age and body of the Time, his form and pressure."

The expression was intended as a local hit, a localism, or as Dr. Furness remarked to the writer as soon as he heard this explanation suggested, as a "gag." As such it was doubtless taken by the audience. We all know what material composed the audiences who crowded to hear Falstaff. Shakespeare's reputation was at that time made, his fortune was rapidly making, he had attracted the notice of the queen, he was in the fashion. It would be going rather far into the region of conjecture to imagine Sir Edward Coke in the Globe playhouse, the austere judge who despised players and charged grand juries against them as vagrants. But it would be safe to assume the presence of Sir Thomas Egerton, better known as Lord Chancellor Ellesmere. He was a patron of the drama, and a few years after Falstaff's first appearance we find him entertaining the queen at his country seat with a representation of *Othello*.[1]

It does not, therefore, require a violent exercise of the historical imagination to place Egerton or Ellesmere in Falstaff's audience. Nor is there any special reason for supposing the absence of Popham, or Croke, or Dodridge, or Crew, or

[1] Camp. Lives Chan. ch. xlviii.

Montague, or Yelverton, or even Bacon himself. If Falstaff had aimed one of his sly winks in the direction of either of these learned persons when he swore that if the Prince and Poins were not arrant cowards there was "no equity stirring," the hit would have been enjoyed by those learned persons no less than by the audience at large. No intelligent spectator of average information could have failed to catch the point at once and with relish.

Taking the primary sense of the words, "no equity stirring," as equivalent to "*no justice going*," the joke is a fairly good joke when explained, but it must be admitted that, like the physical Falstaff himself, it is a trifle heavy. It was not one of his side-splitting jokes. While we cannot accept Mr. Donnelly's condemnation of the expression as forced and unnatural, we can well see that as a witticism it could hardly have succeeded alone in bringing down the house. Letting that stand, however, for all it is worth, the moment you are clearly made to perceive the pointed side allusion to a local topic, the words flash and sparkle with life. Imagine yourself in the audience, knowing all they knew, feeling all they felt, and the words "equity stirring" strike the ear with explosive snap. They were the words the dramatist selected to stir the hands and feet of his audience, and a still more ludicrous application will be suggested farther on.

CHAPTER IV

DATES AND COMMENTATORS

The question of dates. — Silence of commentators accounted for. — Blackstone's misleading dictum. — Darkness of historians. — Light from Coke's Institutes.

NOTWITHSTANDING the pathetic protest of a clever and saucy Irish adventuress against *dates*,[1] it is to be noted that the element of *time* here is of the essence. From first to last it will be found that the whole argument turns upon a succession of heretofore unsuspected coincidences of dates.

There will be found appended[2] a condensed synoptic view of the historic war between the courts, giving the dates of its successive stages and material incidents. The genesis of the controversy is traced to the great struggle between the laws of England and Rome from the twelfth century to the fourteenth, when it merges into the long contest with the constantly developing jurisdiction of chancery, settled finally by the intervention of King James I. on the side of

1 "What has a woman to do with dates?" (Lady Morgan's Memoirs, i. 2.)

2 Appendix A.

chancery in 1616. An attentive examination of this brief and the authorities cited will be found to supersede the necessity for much comment.

The first part of *Henry IV.* was entered at Stationers' Hall, 25 February, 1597–8. It was first exhibited upon the stage during the year 1597. The great explosion, which as Lord Campbell says, "shook Westminster Hall to its centre," did not occur until 1616, when Lord Coke was punished for his violent opposition to chancery (among other causes) by his removal from the bench. If the play had been produced at the time of this explosion, or shortly thereafter, it can scarcely be doubted that the expression "equity stirring" would have been universally accepted as referring thereto.

The silence of commentators upon this passage has been already adverted to. It is not difficult of explanation.

It is a just remark of Hume that "history, being a collection of facts which are multiplying without end, is obliged to adopt arts of abridgment — to retain the more material events, and to drop all the minute circumstances, which are only interesting during the time, or to the persons engaged in the transactions."

Upon the same principle, the culminating crisis of the long struggle for jurisdiction, marked by conspicuous and striking events, — the direct intervention of the king, the final triumph of equity, the downfall of Lord Coke, — and practically closing the chapter, has been taken as, in a general way, all that is necessary to remember, or at all events as all that history can afford to accommodate, of the controversy itself. This is strikingly illustrated by the treatment given to the subject by Sir William Blackstone, the great type of everything conventional. He gives all the information that he supposes the average lawyer or scholar ought in reason to expect, when he tells them that "in the time of Lord Ellesmere, A. D. 1616 [the date is Blackstone's, but not the italics], *arose* that notable dispute between the courts of law and equity, *set on foot* by Sir Edward Coke, then chief justice of the court of king's bench: whether a court of equity could give relief after or against a judgment at the common law?" and follows that up by a brief narrative of the king's part in the transaction, and of Coke's removal.[1] For the immediate purpose the author had in view, this statement might have been thought by him sufficiently adequate and correct. From the standpoint of general history, we know, absolutely know, the statement to be wholly inadequate, erroneous, and positively misleading. The dispute did not "arise" at the date mentioned, but many years before. It was not "set on foot" by Coke, but by his remote predecessors. The authorities collected in the synoptic note referred to establish this fact beyond all doubt or cavil.

[1] 3 Bl. Com. 53.

Blackstone's view has been followed by elementary writers of reputation.[1] Other writers have with more care and correctness treated the "notable dispute" between Coke and Ellesmere as a mere continuation or revival of the old controversy.[2]

Turning from the professional writers to the historians, we are surprised to find that Hume has nothing whatever to say upon the whole subject, that his predecessor Camden was equally silent, and that Lingard can find space for only a short footnote in the line of Blackstone's misleading statement.

Froude completes his history before the end of Elizabeth, and is too much absorbed in the Spanish Armada to notice the criminal proceedings against a lawyer by the name of Heal, in the same year, 1588, the most famous and stirring of the series of indictments already referred to. Hallam does not, like Blackstone, altogether suppress the "heroes before Agamemnon." He recognizes the "overt opposition from the courts of law" before the time of Coke, but only incidentally, and in rather belittling phrase.[3]

[1] White and Tudor's note to the Earl of Oxford's case, 2 Lead. Ca. Eq. 611; Smith's Pr. of Eq. 623.

[2] 1 Sto. Eq. Jur. sec. 46, 51; 3 Pom. Eq. Jur. sec. 1360; 1 Spenc. Eq. 675; Camp. Lives Chan. i. 357, ch. xxii. *ad fin.*, ii. 386, ch. l.; Haynes's Outlines Eq. 225, 226.

[3] Hallam's Cons. Hist. ch. vi. In collecting material for his Lives of the Chancellors, Lord Campbell was "amazed at the

It is hardly necessary to extend the inquiry. Sufficient appears to account for the fact that *the editors and critics of Shakespeare have all omitted to note the war between the courts as a subsisting, burning controversy at the time when Falstaff first appeared upon the stage.* They cannot justly be blamed for failing to observe what they could not have found in the ordinary books of reference, the standard histories of England, and Blackstone's Commentaries. To censure them for not being on terms of intimacy with Coke's Institutes would certainly be a "cruel and unusual punishment."

And yet it is in Coke's Institutes only that the cases are to be found reported in connected series, which prove that the war was stirring during the period of thirty years preceding the appearance of Falstaff, and *especially stirring at the very time the drama was in course of preparation.* These cases, however, are so severely condensed by Coke that much of their interest is lost unless his bare outlines are filled in from other sources, consisting mostly of obscure and forgotten letters and pamphlets, only to be exhumed by dry and dusty digging.

extreme jejuneness of the historians, especially of Hume." (2 Hardcastle's Life of C. 247.) It will shortly be seen how far Campbell's own work is open to the same observation.

CHAPTER V

THE WAR BETWEEN THE COURTS — HEAL'S CASE

Indictment of Sergeant Heal. — His wealth and prominence. — Stir caused by his prosecution. — Queen Elizabeth personally interferes. — The judges disgraced. — Effect of the incident.

THE most recent of the criminal cases was the indictment of Heal, already mentioned. It was also the most remarkable. Heal was like Shakespeare in one respect; he had several different ways of spelling his name. Coke, Bacon, Ellesmere, Hume, and finally Campbell have all written about him, each with a different orthography. Heal, Heale, Hele, Heele, Heyle, or Hale was a prominent lawyer, a sergeant, a magistrate, a parliament man, an aspirant for the succession to Egerton as master of the rolls. He was even supposed to aspire to the great seal, probably basing his claims to preferment upon the fame he had acquired as a champion of the court of chancery. Much to his disappointment, his ambition was crushed by Ellesmere, who denounced him to Queen Elizabeth as "a most greedy and insatiable taker of excessive fees," a "grasping usurer," one of the very sort the "chancery doth give remedy against," a "notorious ambidexter," taking fees on both sides, to the scandal of the profession, and by these "wicked, vile means grown to great wealth, and puffed up to such extreme pride as to be intolerably insolent and offensive."

Finding his hopes thus effectually extinguished, he writes to Ellesmere 14th November, 1600, to "send the four hundred pounds you owe me." [1]

The practice in the House of Commons of hemming and coughing down obnoxious orators is said to have originated with a speech of Sergeant Heal, advancing such high and extreme notions of the royal prerogative that the House hemmed him down.[2] As king's sergeant he opened the trial of Sir Walter Ralegh, and sat by the side of Coke when Coke called Ralegh "spider of hell." [3] Heal came of a Devonshire family so numerous that at one term of court every member of the grand jury answered to the name, spelled probably in almost as many different ways as there were jurors. He founded a hospital, built a mansion-house at a cost of twenty thousand pounds, and left an immense fortune.[4]

[1] Campbell's Lives Chan. ch. xlviii.

[2] Hume's Hist. of Eng. ch. xlv. note LL.

[3] 2 Howell's State Tr. 4.

[4] Woolrych's Eminent Sergeants. The learned reader who may be interested in knowing more about Sergeant Heal than is to be found in the biographies, will find by the following refer-

This is the portrait of the lawyer who in 1588 was indicted of a *premunire* for procuring for a client a suit in chancery to restrain a judgment at law.

The excitement and stir caused by this criminal proceeding against so conspicuous a member of the bar for simply discharging what he conceived to be his professional obligation is not a matter of imagination, but of historical evidence. It finally "aroused the sceptre of the haughty Elizabeth." She interposed in person, as her successor interposed afterwards, on the side of chancery against the common law. The result was that the judges implicated in the proceeding were sharply admonished (Lord Bacon says "upon their knees"), and the objectionable indictment was quashed upon a conveniently discovered quibble. Notwithstanding the ire of the sovereign, and the humiliation of the court, the latter had still spirit enough left to indorse upon

ences that he was much employed in important causes before his indictment of a *premunire* for procuring an injunction for a client to restrain a judgment at law. Of course, the notoriety gained for him by this prosecution, and the queen's interference in his behalf, increased his business and made his fortune. (Beauchamp *v.* Dale, Cro. Eliz. 20; Carden *v.* Tuck, Ib. 89; Scovel *v.* Cabel, Ib. 89; Martin *v.* Whipper, Ib. 114; Wentworth's case, Moore, 244, 713.) It also appears that he was charged about that time with doing a fraudulent business in land warrants, a charge which he indignantly resented, and for which he recovered the large sum for that day of £100 in a slander suit. (Heale *v.* Giddye, Moore, 695; 1 Anderson, 268.)

the unlucky indictment a special memorandum that "it was overthrown for mistaking a name, and not for the matter."[1]

The gravity of the charge, the cruel penalties attached, the profession of the party, his wealth and prominence, the interposition of the queen, the public reprimand administered to the judges upon their knees, all these circumstances supplied themes for infinite discussion and conspired to make this case of Sergeant Heal one of great celebrity. In less than ten years after this memorable event, and while the judges were still holding the same threat of a *premunire* over suitors in equity, Falstaff — in the presence of audiences to whom the name of Sergeant Heal was as familiar as that of Shakespeare himself; in the presence of the queen, who had interfered in Heal's behalf; in the presence of the chancellor,[2] in support of whose authority Heal had been in jeopardy; probably in the presence of some of the very judges who had been rebuked for instigating the prosecution; and it may well

[1] 3 Inst. 124. Lord Bacon's letter to the king "concerning the *premunire*." (Cabala, Montague's Bacon, xii. 36, 41.) Bacon adds to his account of this case, that "my lord Wray, being then chief justice, slipped the collar and was forborne." There is an entire omission of this incident in Campbell's life of Wray, who notices, however, the subserviency of this judge in all crown matters. (Egerton Papers, 391.)

[2] Understanding the term "chancellor" in its quasi-corporate sense. Sir Nicholas Bromley, then deceased, was the chancellor whose immediate authority was in question.

have been in the presence of Sergeant Heal himself — Falstaff "holds the mirror up to nature," and "shows the very age and body of the time, his form and pressure." "An the Prince and Poins be not two arrant cowards, there 's no *equity stirring*." Imagine yourself walking home with Ellesmere from the play and asking him what he understood by that expression. The chancellor would probably have laughed at you and said: "Why, you must belong to some other age."

CHAPTER VI

THE WAR CONTINUED — THROCKMORTON *v.* FINCH

Injunction bill to restrain an inequitable judgment. — Queen Elizabeth interested to maintain the judgment and jealous of Betty Throckmorton. — She interferes again, this time against the chancellor. — She orders the case referred to the twelve judges. — They all decide against the jurisdiction of equity. — The queen's rapacity. — Remarkable coincidence in dates.

It would be a great mistake to assume that in 1597, when Falstaff made his first appearance upon the stage, there was either peace or truce between the courts. There was not even a lull. The fight was on. The great case of Throckmorton and Finch, after years of litigation in the courts of law, was approaching a crisis in the court of chancery. Queen Elizabeth again interposed, but to an effect quite the contrary to that of her interference in the case of Sergeant Heal. She had a personal interest in the controversy, and that interest happened to be opposed to the jurisdiction of chancery, and identified with the finality of a common law judgment.

The facts in this once celebrated but now forgotten case are very simple, and may be briefly stated. It should be premised that the plaintiff, a relative of Catherine Parr, a relative also, it is said, of Shakespeare himself, through his mother,[1] was a nephew of Sir Nicholas Throckmorton (or Throgmorton), a politician of great consequence in his time (1513–1570), better known to posterity as the hero of one of the most infamous state trials that ever disgraced the English bench in its worst days. He owed his escape to the magnificent intrepidity of his own personal defense, unaided by counsel and deprived of his witnesses. The cowardly partisan ruffians who sat and bullied as his judges were not ashamed to confess their spite by punishing with tyrannical severity the jury who acquitted him. This was under Queen Mary, at the same time that she held her sister Elizabeth a prisoner in the Tower.[2]

Early in Elizabeth's reign the unbounded influence of this statesman secured places under the government for many of his relations, and jobs and favors of various kinds for others.[3] It appears that his nephew Thomas had previously obtained from the crown a valuable lease of old priory land at a moderate rent, conditioned, however, to be void upon non-payment of the rent for forty days after it fell due.

[1] Bowden's Religion of Shakespeare, 66.

[2] Holingshed's Chron. 31–55 ; 1 Howell's State Tr. 1554.

[3] See a pamphlet, bound with Peck's Memoirs of Milton, entitled "Legend of Sir Nicholas Throckmorton."

An accidental default in payment occurred, and the capricious queen failed to show the indulgence that might have been expected. Her reason, such as it was, for this change of temper, will appear farther on. Sternly taking advantage of the technical forfeiture, she treated the lease as absolutely void, and conveyed the inheritance to a third party, who afterwards conveyed to Sir Moyle Finch. Finch then made a new lease, and Finch's lessee sued Throckmorton in the court of exchequer in an action of ejectment.

The result was a total defeat for Throckmorton. The court upheld Finch's title. They decided that by reason of the forfeiture for non-payment of rent to the queen, the title of the queen had become absolute, and with it of course her right to convey the land away. Throckmorton took out a writ of error, but the judgment was finally affirmed in the court of exchequer chamber. Sir Edward Coke was at that time attorney-general, and was of counsel for Finch, representing as well the interest of the queen.

Much to the disgust of Finch, who was congratulating himself upon having at last reached the last hair in the tail of litigation, and very little to the satisfaction of the queen, whose claims had been triumphantly vindicated, and to the absolute horror of Sir Edward Coke as a common lawyer, Throckmorton had the presumption to appeal for relief to the chancellor. Notwithstanding a final judgment against him in the common law court of last resort, and that upon a controverted question of title to real estate, he filed a bill to be relieved against the technical forfeiture, and to be relieved from the effect of the judgment.

There would, of course, be no sort of difficulty in such a case at the present day. But juridical equity was at that time an undeveloped system, and its relief was sparingly granted even as against penalties and forfeitures. The plaintiff in equity was required to show special circumstances of extremity or accident to excuse the forfeiture.[1]

Accordingly, Throckmorton's bill alleged such "apparent matter of equity" (the robbery of a servant on his way to pay the rent), to show that the non-payment of rent was no wilful failure, but the result of unavoidable accident. On behalf of his client, Coke demurred to the bill, thus raising the simple issue that, after judgment at law, equity could not interfere.

It was at this point that Queen Elizabeth interposed her authority. Ellesmere was then lord chancellor, and, in accordance with his well-known principles, had clearly manifested his inclination to overrule the demurrer and sustain his juris-

[1] 1 Spence, Eq. 603, 629, notes.

diction.[1] He certainly had a right to presume that Her Majesty, being an interested party, would keep her hands off, and that at least consistency would restrain her from taking action in the teeth of what she had done in the case of Sergeant Heal, a few years before.

But the queen appears to have taken a special interest in this case, for more than a mere business reason. She also had a woman's reason. And now comes in the romance of the case. A daughter of Sir Nicholas Throckmorton had been one of her maids of honor, and by her imprudent conduct had brought scandal upon the court. No less distinguished a name than that of Sir Walter Ralegh was connected with that of Betty Throckmorton in the affair. Sir Walter was one of Queen Elizabeth's alleged "lovers." Here was a piece of audacious rivalry that could never be forgiven. The virtuous indignation of the "imperial votaress" was hardly appeased by the imprisonment of both culprits in the Tower, and her jealousy was not abated, but rather inflamed, by their subsequent intermarriage.[2]

So, when her attorney-general laid before the

[1] When Lord Ellesmere was made Viscount Brackley, the wits of Westminster Hall, who objected to his interference with the judgments of common law courts, converted the name into *Break-Law*. (Foss's Life of Bacon.)

[2] Aiken's Court of Eliz. ii. 314; Gosse's Life of Ral. 55; Edwards's Life of Ral. i. 135; Birch's Mem. of El. i. 79; 47 Dict. Nat. Biog. 191.

sovereign the state of the case, and gave her plainly to understand that Betty Throckmorton's near kinsman was on the high road to success in Her Majesty's court of chancery, and that unless he could be tripped in some way, the queen and her grantee, Finch, would after all lose their case, the courage of Elizabeth was equal to the occasion. Her policy, however, did not carry her beyond the actual emergency. She knew, as well as Coke knew, how the judges stood upon the question. They were the same judges who had already passed upon the title in the court of exchequer and in the court of exchequer chamber. It was their deliberate and affirmed judgment that the chancellor was inclined to disregard in favor of equity. The royal pleasure was accordingly signified to the chancellor, that the consideration of the demurrer should be referred to all the judges of England.[1]

It was certainly unbecoming in the queen, bad taste, and bad ethics, to intermeddle in her own case, but the reference proposed was not unconstitutional. There was then no such thing as an appeal from the chancellor to the house of lords. In a disputed question of jurisdiction between the chancellor on one side and the courts of law

[1] "Egerton, lord chancellor, delivered his opinion in court that the defendant should answer the bill; and, forasmuch as the case was of great consequence, the consideration of the demurrer was by the queen referred to all the judges of England." 4 Inst. 86.

on the other, it seemed more reasonable that the decision should be left to the twelve judges than to the one-man power of the chancellor.[1]

Ellesmere submitted with the best grace he could to the royal command, and in pursuance thereof passed an order referring the cause to all the judges of England. This order bears date May 28, 1597. For nearly six months the judges held the great question under advisement, during which time there were, as Coke says, "divers hearings and conferences." At that time the judges and barons met for hearing and consultation at Sergeants' Inn, Fleet Street.

It is not to be supposed that this long delay was due to any great difficulty that the judges found in the decision. It was more likely to be occasioned, partly by the practical difficulty of getting them all together from the business of their several courts, and partly by the desire to enhance their own importance by holding the public mind in suspense over a cause of magnitude. As common law judges they were naturally inclined to the common law side. At that

[1] Two or three years later, we find this same Sir Moyle Finch, who appears to have been a favored courtier, resorting to similar tactics to defeat a decree of the chancellor against him in favor of the countess of Southampton. He petitioned the queen to refer the decree to the twelve judges. They resolved against it, and the chancellor was obliged to reverse his own decree. (Per Lord Coke in Wrangham's case in the star chamber. 2 Howell's State Tr. 1075.)

time judges had no fixed salaries. Their compensation depended upon fees paid by suitors, and varied with the number of cases and amount of business. They had, therefore, it has been suggested, a personal interest in preventing interference with their jurisdiction.[1]

Such at least is the mercenary motive imputed by Lord Campbell and Mr. Spence. With all deference to those great authorities, it may yet be doubted whether the whole corps of English judges were much, if at all, controlled by any such beggarly consideration. *Victrix causa Diis placuit, sed victa Catoni.* The cause of the judges is a lost cause, but that is no reason for kicking the under dog in the fight.

What those judges thought they were resisting was the attempted "*rule, supremacy, and sway*" of the chancellor over the courts and juries of the land. And they were right in so thinking. The fact cannot be disguised that supremacy was what the chancellors aimed at, and supremacy was what, by the grace of His Majesty James I., they finally achieved.

The royal commission, with Bacon at its head, whose report the king stamped with his approval in 1616, adroitly inflated the wind-ball that has ever since gone bouncing down the ages, that the chancery "*does not assume to undo the judgment, but only to restrain the corrupt con-*

[1] Camp. Lives Chan. ch. xlvii.; 1 Spence, Eq. 674, note.

science of the party." This palpable sophism, which simply hides substance behind form, has been repeated, automatically, by learned chancellors and text-writers from that day to this. To an independent thinker, the specious technical reasoning that the equity court in no way acts upon the law court, but only upon the suitor enjoined from using its process, appears unworthy of serious consideration. "The real justification for the interference is to be found, not in the technical *modus operandi*, but in the substantially just and necessary nature of the interference itself."[1]

The attitude of the English judges of the sixteenth century is not to be criticised from the modern standpoint. It is to be viewed by the lights of the age. And viewing it by the lights of the age and of preceding ages, those judges were morally justified in resisting what appeared to them as simply a bold usurpation. It is in the very nature of equity to claim supremacy; it is, in fact, its *raison d'être.* In the words of Sir Henry Maine, it "has always answered the description of a body of comparatively novel legal principles, claiming to override the older jurisprudence on the strength of an intrinsic ethical superiority."[2]

The claim of absolute superiority has finally

[1] Haynes's Outlines of Equity, 227.

[2] Maine's Ancient Law, 43.

been established in England by express legislation, *that in all cases of conflict the rules of equity shall prevail.*

The judges of England in the sixteenth century are not to be measured by the standards of Sir Henry Maine and the Judicature Acts, but by the standard of the statute of *premunire* as construed in the Year Books. They acted as they did from a loyal sense of what they honestly believed to be their traditional duty to the common law of England, with its trial by jury, in competition with what a modern lord chancellor has frankly admitted to have been an "upstart and usurping judicature."[1]

They occupied a representative position, and reflected the sentiments and the prejudices of the great mass of the English people.

The history of the struggle (see synoptic note[2]) shows very plainly that the growing power of the chancellor was from an early day viewed with suspicion and alarm. Among the English common people there was a deeply-rooted sentiment of attachment to the English trial by jury, and of aversion to the Roman one-man power of adjudication, even when confined to questions of property. The colonists who settled America largely brought this sentiment with them. They

[1] Lord Cairns, in debate in the House of Lords, 30 April, 1872.

[2] Appendix A.

regarded the common law as their safeguard from oppression, and feared the court of chancery as a possible engine of arbitrary power. In colonial New England and Pennsylvania no similar court was tolerated.[1] This fact illustrates the feeling of the people from whose midst those colonists went forth. This popular sentiment the judges of England had always represented, and still continued to represent. Nothing could be more certain than that a large majority of them would sustain Finch's demurrer. But in order to give to their decision the imposing weight of a finality it was desirable that it should be withheld until it could be made unanimous.

Their decision was at last signified to the chancellor by Chief Justice Popham. The unanimous resolution of the judges was that after judgment the party could not be relieved in equity, as tending to the subversion of the common law, and thereupon they all certified that the demurrer was good, and that Finch ought not to be required to answer. On November 15, 1597, the result was announced by the chancellor in open court, and that ended the case. It did not, however, end the controversy.[2]

[1] Phelps's Jurid. Eq. sec. 17.

[2] In Coke's Institutes and in Cro. Jac. will be found three several reports of the case of Throckmorton *v.* Finch, as given upon the authority of Lord Coke himself. (3 Inst. 124 ; 4 Inst. 86 ; Courtney *v.* Glanvil, Cro. Jac. 344.) In a tract styled "Jurisdiction of Chancery Vindicated," appearing as an appen-

Attention is now called to the interesting and significant fact, never before noted, that *in a little more than three months after the last-mentioned date, the First Part of Henry the Fourth was entered upon the books of the Stationers' Company.*

In view of the importance and historical significance of this case of Throckmorton *v.* Finch, it is not apparent why it should have been so universally slighted by modern text-writers. In its preliminary stages in the courts of common law (the courts of exchequer and exchequer chamber)

dix to 1 Rep. Chan., also printed, and more correctly, in the first volume of Collectanea Juridica (p. 72), may be found quite another version of the same case, differing from Coke's in some essential particulars. This volume of reports (1 Rep. Ch.) is anonymous, and is characterized by Lord Hardwicke as "of no authority," and by Chancellor Kent as "loose, meagre, and inaccurate, of not much weight or authority." (3 Atkyns, 334; 1 Wilson, 162; 1 Kent, Com. 492.) The appendix is also anonymous. The supposition of Mr. Spence, that the author of this tract was Lord Ellesmere (1 Spence, Eq. 683, note), is a palpable error, unless we admit that Ellesmere wrote it after his own death. Not only is the death of Lord Ellesmere distinctly referred to (1 Coll. Jur. 19), but the paper shows on its face that it was not written until after the death of Coke, who survived Ellesmere nearly twenty years. In every particular of variance I have followed Coke, in preference to this anonymous and prejudiced, although learned, writer. I have, however, taken some of his statements and dates, not inconsistent with Coke's, to fill up Coke's meagre outline. This case has been altogether overlooked by Lord Campbell, both in his life of Ellesmere and in his life of Coke, although among modern writers he is not exceptional in that respect. The same remark is applicable as well to Heal's case.

it is detailed with unusual fullness by nearly all the contemporary reporters.[1]

The case shows up the revolting rapacity of Queen Elizabeth in enforcing the technical forfeiture of a lease for a single and accidental non-payment of rent within the limited period. Before the next pay-day the rent in arrear was paid in full, and an acquittance given by the queen's receiver, and all future installments were promptly paid and acquittances given.

Notwithstanding all this, and the lapse of twenty-one years, the queen had the conscience and the heart to enforce the stale forfeiture by selling the land clear of the lease, and in this suit with her grantee the court felt itself obliged to hold, under the harsh law which then prevailed, that by the mere non-payment of rent at the day, the lease, by its own limitation, became absolutely void, and what was void could not be made good by the subsequent payment and acquittance.

It is not at all surprising that Lord Ellesmere (who, by the way, as solicitor-general, had argued strenuously on the queen's side in the court of exchequer chamber) should, when chancellor, have felt it his duty to prevent, by injunction, such monstrous injustice, and it was again characteristic of Elizabeth to forestall his action by

[1] Popham, 25, 53; 1 Anderson, 303; Moore, 291; 2 Leonard, 134; Cro. Eliz. 222.

referring the case to the same judges who had been the willing instruments of its perpetration.[1]

[1] Referring to the great *lapse of time* in this case between the forfeiture and its enforcement, Manwood, chief baron of the exchequer, in the course of his elaborate judgment (in law French) said: —

"Of the private owner the law requires vigilance, for the law will not be more vigilant for him than he is for himself. But in the case of the queen, the law itself is vigilant for the queen, and requires of her no exercise of diligence, and imputes to her no laches or folly, but charges subjects with notice of her title, and warns them to avoid possession where the queen is entitled."

Referring to the forfeiture, and its effect, *ipso facto*, without "inquisition of office" to enable the queen to grant the land, clear of the lease, the same judge continued: —

"The lease being determined, both in law (*droit*), in estate, in privity, and in property, the land was at the ample disposition of the queen, without office and before office."

It had been urged for Throckmorton that *no demand* had been made for the rent unpaid. To this point the learned chief baron replied: —

"It is the tenant's duty to pay or tender, and the queen is not obliged to make demand, as the subject is, for she has tenants infinite, and would have to employ armies of men to demand her rents, if she were obliged to make demand of each tenant."

Not content with capturing the land, the insatiate queen claimed also, and successfully, the *mesne profits* — that is, all that Throckmorton had got from the land, and all that he might, could, or should, with due diligence, have gotten out of it, during the twenty-one years that he was regularly paying his rent to the queen's receiver, and getting acquittances, from the time of the forfeiture to the time of its enforcement. It will interest modern readers (laymen as well as lawyers) to note with what easy grace an English law court of the sixteenth century was able to swallow such a tough proposition.

Manwood, chief baron (again): —

"The lease was void before office, and the grant over of the land good before office. The office found after the grant over was effectual to inform the queen of the avoidance, so as to entitle her to the *mesne profits* accruing between the avoidance and the grant over." (Moore, 295; 2 Leonard, 134, 143.)

CHAPTER VII

CASES COMPARED

Heal's case and Throckmorton *v.* Finch compared. — Effect on Falstaff's public. — How they understood "equity stirring."

The once important but now forgotten case of Throckmorton *v.* Finch has been revived in some detail in order to enable the learned reader to decide for himself whether or not Falstaff's original audiences must have been aware of that litigation, and of the state of the controversy between the courts which its pendency indicated.

Take this case in connection with that of Sergeant Heal a few years before. Here are two cases, one a criminal prosecution of a prominent lawyer, the other a civil case involving an interest of the queen; both are cases of a conflict of jurisdiction between law and equity; both are made famous by the personal interposition of the sovereign; both are made more conspicuous from the apparent inconsistency of her dealing; in one case, the judges are publicly disgraced for interfering with the chancellor; in the other, they are publicly invited to overrule the chancellor; in other words, both are cases of first-class magnitude, importance, and contemporary renown, although of no twentieth-century significance, and long since relegated, both of them, to the lumber-room of back numbers and dead issues. But the question is not what impression the controversy makes upon this generation. We are talking now about puff-sleeved gentlemen with peaked starched beards, who wore doublet and slashed hose, who went to the play sporting rapiers, with roses on their shoes and plumes in their hats. We are dealing with a time when the nobility lived in Drury Lane, when Islington was a suburban village, and when the spikes of London Bridge were decorated with human heads. To understand Shakespeare we will have to borrow a little from the magic of his fancy, call up the dead of three centuries ago, and resurrect the sentiments and the quarrels that were buried with them.[1] An effort of the historical imagination will enable us to realize the state of mind of Falstaff's public in relation to the great struggle of equity against the rigor of the law, of which the case of Heal and the case of Throckmorton are to-day the speaking witnesses. We shall have no difficulty in perceiving that when, in 1597, Falstaff was heard exclaiming that if the prince and

[1] "L'histoire n'est que l'histoire du cœur; nous avons à chercher les sentiments des générations passées, et nous n'avons à chercher rien autre chose." (Taine, Hist. Lit. Ang. v. 255.)

Poins were not arrant cowards there was "no equity stirring," everybody who had sense enough to want to go to the play at all had the common intelligence to see at once the palpable allusion to the militant equity of the court of chancery, the equity that was fighting its way over the prejudices, the jealousy, and the obstinacy of the courts of law.

CHAPTER VIII

COMPARED WITH SHAKESPEARE *v.* LAMBERT

Throckmorton case analogous to Shakespeare *v.* Lambert, pending in chancery at the same time. — Shakespeare's business interest in "equity" while producing Falstaff. — Startling coincidence in dates.

It is conceived that no Shakespearian scholar will want to hear argument upon such a point as the presumed knowledge by the dramatist himself of such a case as that last referred to. But it so happens that, apart from the violent presumption arising from his marvelous general information, especially as to all matters connected with the courts, there is authentic evidence of a more pointed and personal character. Reference might be made here to the significant fact that, fresh from the study of the consecutive reigns of Richard II. and Henry IV., Shakespeare must have been much impressed by the conflict between equity and the common law, which was a salient feature, if not the dominant note, of the whole period (see synoptic note [1]). But without dwelling upon that consideration, there is at hand

[1] Appendix A.

matter more closely in point. Laying no stress upon the fact heretofore adverted to, of Throckmorton's relationship to Shakespeare, through the Ardens, I refer to the chancery suit of Shakespeare *v.* Lambert, pending in 1597, and for several years before and after. There will be occasion, farther on, to develop the particulars of that litigation, under another head. It will be seen that the object of that suit was the redemption of a mortgage upon his mother's maiden property, after alleged legal forfeiture, and that its circumstances were so nearly analogous in principle to those of Throckmorton *v.* Finch that the progress of the last-named case could not have failed to arrest the closest attention of Shakespeare and his counsel. It will further be seen that the Shakespeares *changed front and filed a new bill against Lambert, on November 24, 1597, nine days after the decision of the judges was announced in Throckmorton* v. *Finch*, a startling coincidence in dates, now for the first time noted. And it will appear upon the whole as a reasonable inference from all the facts in evidence, that during the period of six months, from May to November, 1597, that the case of Throckmorton *v.* Finch was under advisement, at the instance of the queen, by the twelve judges of England, Shakespeare was in consultation with his lawyers respecting the new move about to be made in the court of chancery in the case of Shakespeare *v.* Lambert. That Shakespeare's counsel were aware of the pendency and bearing of such a case, every lawyer will admit, and indeed it would be ridiculous to doubt. And that Shakespeare extracted from his lawyers all that they knew that was worth his knowing it would be rather bold to deny, in the face of what is known of his powers of absorption, his shrewd business talent, his interest in legal matters generally, and his special interest in the particular subject-matter. Thus opportunity combines with motive, and both with genius, to make the inference irresistible. The case of Throckmorton *v.* Finch as a possible precedent to the case of Shakespeare *v.* Lambert was brought home to Shakespeare, and was pressing upon his eager attention, *while he was either actually engaged in the composition of the drama, or while the unpublished MS. was still in his hands, subject to revision.* Of the two alternatives thus suggested, the former is the one which more nearly coincides with the generally received opinion as to the probable period of composition.[1]

[1] The play of *Richard II.* was entered at Stationers' Hall in August, 1597, and the First Part of *Henry IV.* in the ensuing February. It is hence supposed that the last-named play was put into its present shape between those dates, although, of course, the mere entry for publication is no proof that the play might not, in some shape, have been performed previously. It is true that in the ninth edition of Outlines (i. 153) the appearance on the stage of the First Part of *Henry IV.* is "confidently assigned to the spring of year 1597." No direct evidence is

But, upon either hypothesis, a flood of light is let in upon Falstaff's allusion to "*equity stir-*

claimed in support of this rather dogmatic statement, which, upon examination, turns out to be merely an inference from the known facts, that the drama had been exhibited in public before the name of Oldcastle had been altered to that of Falstaff, and that this change was made in or before February, 1598. (Outlines, ii. 349, 350.) The only additional circumstance adduced to narrow the time of production down to the spring of 1597 is the death of Lord Cobham, March 5, 1597. (Ib. ii. 350, note 261.) Upon investigation, however, it will be found by those interested in bringing this matter down to a fine point, that the only possible effect of the death of Cobham, as a piece of circumstantial evidence, is as tending to show that at all events the First Part of *Henry IV.* with the obnoxious name of Oldcastle "thoughtlessly introduced into the comedy," could not have been exhibited *prior* to March, 1597, but is no evidence whatever as to the particular time of the production of the piece *after* that date. The conjecture of Halliwell-Phillipps, that the comedy was represented before the queen in the Christmas holidays of 1597–98 (Outlines, i. 153), is probably correct. It coincides with the conclusion of Stokes, who assigns the date of production to the end of the year 1597. (Sto. Chron. Order, 54.) There is certainly not a particle of proof, either direct or inferential, that the play had ever been publicly represented before. In fact, the only thing at all certain about the whole matter is the *date of publication*, 25th of February, 1597–98, and that the text of the first quarto (1598, reproduced in Bankside edition) is "so complete and perfect that it must have been printed from Shakespeare's MS. or a very accurate copy thereof." (Intro. to Bank. ed. *1 H. IV.*) All beyond that is mere conjecture or inference from very meagre and unsatisfactory data. The mention by Francis Meres, in Palladis Tamia, 1598, relied on by Furnivall (see his introduction to Gervinus), obviously amounts to nothing as original evidence, since we have the authentic date of publication in February of that same year. In this connection the writer takes occasion to commend to all future editors, commentators and critics a close study of the three contemporaneous cases referred to in the text, with their instructive coincidences *ring.*" Plainly, it is the equity of the court of chancery that was stirring the attorney-general, stirring the queen, stirring the palace, stirring the twelve judges of England, stirring the bar, and stirring the public. It was the same equity of the court of chancery that was at the same time stirring Shakespeare's lawyers, stirring Shakespeare the business man, and thus stirring Shakespeare the playwright. The conclusion goes of itself. It was the same juridical equity, the equity of the court of chancery at war with the courts of law, that was stirring Falstaff and stirring Falstaff's audience. It was this special, local, and transient application to a subject of contemporaneous interest, and not the broader and tamer signification of the word "equity" as equivalent to "justice," that winged the shaft, and made the sally a success. No one knew better than the playwright who wrote it, that

> "A jest's prosperity lies in the ear
> Of him that hears it, never in the tongue
> Of him that makes it."
> (*Love's Labour's Lost*, Act V. scene 2.)

of dates, viz.: Throckmorton *v.* Finch, Mylward *v.* Weldon (to be cited presently), and Shakespeare *v.* Lambert, with the suggestion that from the circumstances of these cases and the authentic record dates they furnish there may possibly be extracted a more satisfactory clue to the approximate time of production of the play in question than have been found in any data hitherto available, when those circumstances and dates are read in the light of Falstaff's "*no equity stirring.*"

CHAPTER IX

BACON AND HIS CULT

The word "stirring" used by Bacon in same connection. — Parallelisms considered. — Dissimilarity of style. — The Baconian cult incidentally exploded by the Lambert litigation in the light of "equity stirring."

THE peculiar aptness of the word "stirring" to make a picturesque impression of the agitation incident to the great struggle of courts over their jurisdiction is too plain for comment. Nevertheless, it may be worth notice that the same word is repeatedly used by Lord Bacon in precisely the same connection, and applied to precisely the same subject-matter. It occurs in his remarkable letter to King James I. of February 21, 1615–16, "concerning the *premunire* in the king's bench against the chancery," already referred to.[1] In this letter he places before the king a very clear statement of the controversy, from the equity standpoint. He cites the statute of *premunire*, 27 Edw. III., and the statute of prohibition, 4 Henry IV.; argues that they were aimed only against foreign, that is, the

[1] Cabala, Montague's Bacon, xii. 36, 41; *ante*, pp. 35, 36.

ecclesiastical, courts; refers to the attempt lately made in the king's bench to bring these statutes to bear against the court of chancery, by indicting suitors therein; offers the insidious suggestion that Lord Coke is not to be disgraced "*at this time;*" then suggests "the public affront to your high court of chancery (which is the court of your absolute power)," and that use should be made thereof "to settle your authority and strengthen your prerogative;" continues, that nothing is more useful "than upon a just and fit occasion to make some example against the presumption of a judge in causes that concern your majesty, whereby the whole body of these magistrates may be contained to better awe," and recommends that the same course be pursued as was taken in Queen Elizabeth's time, in the case of Sergeant Heal, already referred to. This characteristic letter is introduced by an account of a recent interview between the writer and Lord Chancellor Ellesmere, then sick and supposed to be on his deathbed. "I did not fail in my conjecture (writes Bacon) that this business of the chancery hath *stirred* him." And again he writes: "If any of the puisne judges did *stir this business*, I think that judge worthy to lose his place."[1]

Bacon notices that "this business of the chancery" had *stirred* Ellesmere. Falstaff, quite as

[1] Bacon's Works, xii. 36.

naturally, alludes to the same business as stirring things generally.[1]

It is upon parallelisms of thought and expression like that cited, many of which may be found in the writings of Bacon and Shakespeare, that the work of the dramatist has been, by some modern theorists, attributed to the philosopher. That interesting and somewhat mysterious problem does not fall, so far, within the scope of this argument. The line of investigation now being developed was entered upon with entire indifference as to whether the real author was named Bacon, or Shakespeare, or Jacques-Pierre, or Jack-Peter. As it progressed, however, a side view of that question was opened up, incidentally.

If Bacon, the jurist, is admitted to be the author of the play, the use of the word "equity" in its juridical sense instantly becomes too obvious to talk about, and much of the argument might be spared. The strongest point for the cipher theory (if theory it may be called) is made upon this play and upon the very act in which occurs the expression "no equity stirring." The striking repetition of the word "*bacon*," the

[1] The same word will be found used in the same connection, by a learned chancery reporter, in a valuable note upon this subject of disputed jurisdiction which goes over the whole ground. He says: "Within a few years after Lord Coke's death, the question of equitable jurisdiction was again *stirred*, and, as it seems, not wholly without success." (2 Swanston's Rep. 26, note.)

remarkably frequent repetition of the word "*Francis*," the introduction of the word "*Nicholas*" (the name of Francis Bacon's father), and the introduction of the word "*equity*" (Nicholas Bacon having also been chancellor) are certainly curious coincidences with the mysterious expression: "We have the receipt of fern-seed, *we walk invisible*." When, in addition to all this, we find the word "*equity*" here properly used in its technical sense, just as any lawyer would have used it, and with reference to the very controversy in which Bacon himself afterwards became a prominent actor, it must be conceded that the array is altogether too formidable to be treated with contempt. The difficulty which Mr. Donnelly found in the expression is at once removed.[1] So far from the phrase "no equity stirring" being dismissed as "forced and unnatural," he should cling to it as the king-pin of the wain.

On the other hand, there remains here, as in every part of the controversy, the stubborn fact of the essential dissimilarity of style. Not one of the parallelisms cited, marvelous though they may be supposed as coincidences of thought and expression, nor all of them together, can satisfy the unbiased mind that the philosopher possessed the "trick" of the dramatist, nor that it was possible for Bacon to have produced Falstaff, any

[1] Great Cryptogram, 524.

more than it was possible for Shakespeare to have produced the Novum Organum.

In addition, we have the special light thrown upon the question by the pending chancery suit of Shakespeare *v.* Lambert. In the condition of that case at the time the First Part of *Henry IV.* was in preparation, already adverted to and to be more fully developed later, we have notice that the practical subject of court equity was at that precise juncture pressing upon the attention of this same William Shakespeare as a matter of urgent business. In this circumstance we find a finger-post that points directly to the man of Stratford as the writer of this particular drama. But this particular drama, as has just been pointed out, is the stronghold of the Baconian cult. Once let it be admitted that the personal and business relations of the man of Stratford to the practical subject of court equity, through the pending chancery litigation against Lambert, had anything to do with suggesting the contemporaneous allusion to "equity stirring," and the Baconian cult is incidentally, though none the less effectually, exploded.

CHAPTER X

POSSIBLE OBJECTIONS

Partisan bias. — Anachronism. — Irrelevance. — Failure to impress posterity.

It may be said that as a politic playwright, anxious to keep on good terms with all sides, Shakespeare seldom mixes with the controversies of his day.

There are two somewhat opposite views that may be taken here, according to the construction, or, rather, according to the delicate shade of meaning, that may be placed upon the language. One is, that here was a rare opportunity for a catching side allusion, perfectly good-humored, and without partisan color. The struggle against the constantly growing power of the chancellor was not an ephemeral or an isolated phenomenon, but was simply one phase of the secular contest with absolutism, which, at the time when Shakespeare wrote, was girding itself for the approaching civil war. Any allusion to any phase of that struggle was sure to touch a popular chord, and here we find the dramatist, with his usual non-partisan dexterity, while boldly striking the chord, preserving at the same time his neutrality, without offense to either side. The equivocal meaning of the term "equity" was his opportunity. The risky allusion, if it was risky, was prudently veiled under a broader and absolutely harmless significance.

On the other hand, it may be thought, and possibly with reason, that the delicate balance of neutrality is not altogether maintained, and that the somewhat boastful appeal to equity as a thing "stirring" betrays a bias towards the chancellor's side of the controversy. If that be the case, it would be perfectly in keeping with the character of Sir John Falstaff, a knight, an aristocrat, and a prince's companion. He would have no sympathy with the popular principles upon which the opposition to chancery was based. Neither, for that matter, had Shakespeare himself. He had, in fact, little sympathy with the masses, their interests, or their rights.

This point has been often noticed. It has been aptly said that nowhere in any of his writings is there "a hint of sympathy with personal rights as against the sovereign, nor with parliament, then first assuming a protective attitude toward the English people, nor with the few judges who, like Coke, showed a glorious obstinacy in their resistance to the prerogative. In all his works there is not one direct word for liberty of speech, thought, religion,—those rights which, in his age, were the very seeds of time, into which his eyes, of all men, could best look to see which grain would grow and which would not." [1]

"Had Shakespeare cared for the people, their liberties, their rights and interests, surely he might have put into the mouth of one of his eight or nine hundred characters a statement, hint, or suggestion to that effect." [2]

On the other hand, he seldom misses an opportunity to show contempt for the vulgar. Rarely is "first citizen" or "second citizen" introduced, except to figure as a churl or a clown. Familiar specimens will at once occur to the scholar of the countless phrases in which the "hempen homespuns," the "crew of patches," "rude mechanicals that work for bread," "knaves that smell of sweat," "multiplying spawn," "herd of broils and plagues," "you common cry of curs," in short, the every-day, working masses, "the tag-rag people," are treated with aristocratic scorn.

Actors and playwrights in those days naturally courted the nobility, and to the peerage Shakespeare looked for friends and patrons. His weakness for aristocracy was betrayed in the efforts he was making at or about the very time now in question to secure for his father a herald's coat of

[1] Davis's The Law in Shakespeare, 34.
[2] Morgan's Shakespeare, 243.

arms and a patent of gentility. It has already been pointed out that in the war between the court of chancery and the courts of law, the sympathies of the aristocracy and their dependents were naturally inclined to the equity side. Moreover, the property interests of the Shakespeare family were directly involved in the dispute. The chancery suit of Shakespeare *v.* Lambert must be allowed its weight in determining a bias towards the success of equity in the struggle.

There may, therefore, be good reason for entertaining the opinion that upon this occasion the author could well afford to throw off his habitual reserve, and in the character of Sir John somewhat boastfully allude to the progress which equity, the favorite of the court party, was making in its struggle for supremacy over the common law, with its trial by jury, the bulwark of popular rights.

No Shakespearian scholar will object that it was an *anachronism* to attribute to the time of Henry IV. an allusion to events of a century or two later.[1] It curiously happens, however, that there is in reality no anachronism here, as will be seen by the authorities cited in the note so

[1] Shakespeare's plays abound with anachronisms, and "there is not a single play which does not reflect, in every act, almost, some feature of the age of Elizabeth." (Corson, Int. to Sh., 27, 28.) Rather a strong way of putting it.

often referred to.[1] The reign of Henry IV. was one in which equity was stirring in a most lively manner. The court of chancery was making vigorous efforts to strengthen and expand its jurisdiction, and its encroachments, as they were called, were alarming the people and provoking the opposition of parliament. One of the evidences of that opposition is the statute of prohibition of Henry IV. This act, in connection with the statute of *premunire* of 27 Edw. III., afforded the common law judges a basis for their controversy with the chancellors, respecting the absolute finality of judgments. It is hardly worth while to dwell upon this point, further than to note the coincidence for what it may be worth.

Possibly it may be something of a disappointment to us moderns, who hold no stock in this rather mouldy quarrel, and can at best get up no more than a languid antiquarian interest in it, to find ourselves obliged to brush away three centuries of dust in order to perceive what appears to be the merest localism, altogether aside from the march and movement of the play. Possibly we had rather not find it so. The venerable gag throws no light upon the Gadshill incident, into the very crisis of which it is interjected. Except so far as it shows him a man of the world, in full touch with the very age and body of the time,

[1] Appendix A.

it brings us no closer to the true inwardness of the naughty, funny, fat old knight, nor does it tend to illustrate his shady relations with Prince Hal. In this respect it is like the "wild duck" which wings its flight across the stage a second later. These are the "favors," not the steps or figures, of the cotillion. Those who had them to handle knew what they were. And we may as well remember, all along, that *we* did not happen to be the persons, or the generation, primarily in the playwright's mind when he launched the squib. Shakespeare was a poet, but he was a poet who meant business. He made plays for money, and he made them to *go*.

"However repugnant it may be to the flowing sentiments of the æsthetic critics, no doubt can arise in the minds of those who will listen to evidence that when Pope asserted that —

> 'Shakespeare, whom you and every play-house bill
> Style the divine, the matchless, what you will,
> For gain, not glory, winged his roving flight
> And grew immortal in his own despight,'

he not only expressed the traditional belief of his own day, but one which later researches have unerringly verified." [1]

It is in fact a doubtful question whether he much courted posthumous fame. So far as we know him personally, he certainly did not *act* as if he did, however various the sentiments he may

1 Outlines, i. 163.

have put in the mouths of the characters he invented. What he seems principally to have had in view when he made plays was the current coin of the realm and the live persons who had it in their pockets; and his primary object was to extract that coin from those pockets and transfer it to his own, for an honest equivalent. He noticed that those live people very much enjoyed a gag, once in a while, and were willing to pay for it, and gags he gave them. And he did it conscientiously, and upon an avowed principle. The principle was that players were and "are the abstract and brief chronicles of the time," and that the purpose of playing was, and is, to show "the very age and body of the time, his form and pressure." [1]

[1] It was upon this principle that he gagged and squibbed, in *Twelfth Night*, this same Sir Edward Coke, who figures so largely in this narrative. Coke, as attorney-general, made himself sublimely ridiculous by his vulgar abuse of Sir Walter Ralegh, when prosecuting him for treason. After a free use of the pronoun "thou" in connection with such epithets as monster, viper, etc., he turns on Ralegh ferociously, with the silly explanatory outburst, which, unfortunately for the great lawyer's reputation, has become immortal, "For I *thou* thee, thou traitor!" (2 Howell's State Tr. 4.) Shakespeare, catching the humor of the scene, makes Sir Toby Belch say, in giving suggestions to Sir Andrew Aguecheek for his challenge, "If thou *thou'st* him some thrice, it shall not be amiss; and as many lies as will lie in thy sheet of paper." (*Twelfth Night*, Act III. scene 2.) It was thus that Shakespeare the actor, in behalf of his craft, "got even" with the judge who incited grand jurors to indict players as vagrants and a public nuisance. It was thus that Shakespeare the playwright illustrates the truth of Hamlet's opinion about

In contemplating and appraising the immediate but transient effect of localisms upon the audiences for whom they were designed, it must be remembered that it is altogether impossible to reproduce precisely the same effect upon ourselves.[1] Long after the exhibition of fireworks, we go over the field in broad daylight and pick up a burnt-out rocket. That is all we see of it, and the difference between us and those who were dazzled by its flight is simply the difference of an interjection. We say "Oh!" but we do not say "*Ah!*" with a big A, long drawn out.

Here we have an expression that does not need to be construed by the context. It glitters alone. Like a meteor, it shines by its own light. But, like a meteor, it must be within the range of vision to be known for what it is. The size and brilliancy of the phenomenon vary inversely with the distance of the observer. To those near, in time as in place, the effect is startling; the varied colors are boldly distinguishable, the luminous train is clearly cut upon the sky. To the remote observer, there is only a faint and ghostly

players, and applies the words to Coke: "After your death you were better have a bad epitaph, than their ill report while you live." (*Hamlet*, Act II. scene 2.) Appendix D.

[1] "Pleines de vie, de sens, de vérité pour les peuples qui les ont animées de leur souffle, elles ne sont plus à nos yeux que des lettres mortes, des hiéroglyphes scellés, elles ne sont plus pour nous qu'un objet de curieuse analyse." (Renan, Etudes.)

gleam, coming up out of the infinitude of nothing, and instantly vanishing in the same dark abyss. To those who do not or will not look, the apparition does not exist.

CHAPTER XI

THE COMIC ELEMENT — MYLWARD *v.* WELDON

A practical object-lesson in "equity stirring." — Its ludicrous effect on Falstaff's public. — Supplies the necessary comic element. — Combines with Throckmorton's case to impress all classes. — Why this case has escaped attention. — Failure of Campbell and others to perceive connection with Falstaff.

It will be remembered that at the outset the burden was assumed not only of showing that in the passage quoted the term "equity" was used in a secondary sense as referring to juridical equity, but further, that it was used in this sense with a "*twofold application.*" The attempt has been made to point out an allusion to what Bacon calls "this business of the chancery," — *the warfare between the courts of law and equity,* — with what degree of success the intelligent reader, who will take the pains to verify the citations, will judge for himself. Before passing from this branch of the subject, there is another striking coincidence in dates to be noted, and another remarkable case to be cited; a case absolutely unique; a case which will probably be conceded to establish beyond all question the allusion to juridical or court equity, quite independently of the controversy referred to; while, at the same time, it will be recognized at sight as the indispensable comic ingredient to flavor Falstaff's "play to the galleries" with an irresistibly ludicrous association.

The notable case referred to is the chancery suit of Mylward *v.* Weldon.[1]

Campbell, in his life of Ellesmere, introduces this case as follows: "We have on record a very striking instance of the vigor with which he (Lord Chancellor Ellesmere) strove to correct the prolixity of the written pleadings in his court." After citing the effective part of the chancellor's preposterous and ludicrous order, the only comment which occurred to the learned biographer is the following: "The order should have gone on to require that a print of the unlucky Richard, with his head peeping through the volumes of sheepskin, should, *in terrorem*, be hung up in the chambers of every equity draughtsman."

The case is referred to by Mr. Spence in that part of his valuable treatise devoted to the early procedure of the court of chancery, for the purpose of illustrating the following proposition in his text: "Very stringent measures were taken to prevent impertinent matter from being introduced into answers, and other subsequent plead-

[1] 1 Spence, Eq. 376, note *h;* Campbell's Lives of the Chancellors, ch. xlvii.

ings,[1] of which the orders at the foot will serve as sufficient illustrations." Upon examination, "*the orders at the foot*" are found to be orders passed on two different days in this one case, and as this case is of a character to lay a considerable tax upon modern credulity, and none other like it is cited, it is necessary to reproduce the whole of Mr. Spence's footnote.

"The following have [2] been selected as calculated to give some notion of the despotic authority which was exercised by the court on the subject.

"Between William Mylward, Plaintiff,
William Weldon and others, Defendants,
And between William Weldon, Plaintiff,
and William Mylward, Defendant. 8th February, 1596.[3]

"'And where Richard Mylward, the plaintiff's son, did confess that he himself did heretofore draw the long replications (*sic*) of six score sheets of paper, which heretofore was put into the court by the plaintiff to the answer of the defendants; in which replication much impertinent and idle matter was inserted, as it heretofore seemed to his Lordship, of purpose to put the defendants to extraordinary charges, and that he used no advice of counsel therein: It is ordered by his Lordship that the said Richard Mylward be forthwith committed to the prison of the Fleet for his misdemeanor and abuse offered to this court.' Reg. Lib. A, 1596, fol. 667.

"Same cause, 10th February, 1596.[4]

"'For as much as it now appeared to this court by a report made by the now Lord Keeper, being then Master of the Rolls,[5] upon consideration had of the plaintiff's Replication according to

[1] By the modern practice, all "subsequent pleadings," such as special replications and rejoinders, are dispensed with, and their place supplied by the liberal allowance of amendments.

[2] The use of the plural here is somewhat misleading. As stated above, there is but one case in question.

[3] Mr. Spence fails to notice that the date was *Old Style*, a neglect which leads him into an error, as will be seen later on, in the name of the responsible chancellor.

[4] The learned author again neglects to notice O. S.

[5] Egerton, afterwards Lord Ellesmere, not Puckering, as afterwards erroneously stated.

an order of the 7th of May, of Anno 37 Reginæ,[1] that the said Replication doth amount to six score sheets of paper, and yet all the matter thereof which is pertinent might have been well contrived in sixteen sheets of paper, wherefore the plaintiff was appointed to be examined to find out who drew the same Replication, and by whose advice it was done, to the end that the offender might, for example's sake, not only be punished, but also be fined to her Majesty for that offence, and that the defendant might have his charges sustained thereby (the execution of which order was, by a later order made by the late Lord Keeper [2] the 26th of June, Anno 37th Reginæ, suspended without any express cause, shewed thereof in that order, and was never since called upon until the matter came to be heard on Tuesday last before the Lord Keeper [3] at which time some mention was again made of the same Replication), and for that it now appeared to his Lordship, by the confession of Richard Mylward, alias Alexander, the plaintiff's son, that the said Richard himself did both draw, devise, and engross the same Replication, and because his Lordship is of opinion that such an abuse is not in any sort to be tolerated — proceeding of a malicious purpose to increase the defendant's charge, and being fraught with much impertinent matter not fit for the court: *It is therefore ordered that the warden of the Fleet shall take the said Richard Mylward into his custody and shall bring him into Westminster Hall on Saturday about* 10 *of the clock in the forenoon, and then and there* SHALL CUT A HOLE *in the midst of the said engrossed Replication, which is delivered unto him for that purpose,* AND PUT THE SAME RICHARD'S HEAD THROUGH THE SAME HOLE, *and so let the same Replication hang about his shoulders, with the written side outward, and then, the same so hanging, shall lead the said Richard bareheaded and barefaced round about Westminster Hall, whilst the courts are sitting,* AND SHALL SHOW HIM AT THE BAR OF EVERY OF THE THREE COURTS *within the Hall, and then shall take him back again to the Fleet, and keep him prisoner until he shall have paid* £10, *to her Majesty for a fine, and* 20 *nobles to the defendant for his costs in respect of the aforesaid abuse, which fine and costs are now adjudged and imposed upon him by this court for the abuse aforesaid.'* Reg. Lib. A, 1596, fol. 672. Sir J. Puckering, Lord Keeper.[4] This order (con-

[1] 7 May, A. D. 1595. [2] Sir John Puckering. [3] Ellesmere.

[4] Mr. Spence is here in error, caused, as already pointed out, by the failure to observe that the date was Old Style.

tinues Mr. Spence) is mentioned by Tothill, but his reference is, as usual, erroneous."

The learned reader may now be safely asked whether the above megacephalic deliverance is not absolutely unique in jurisprudence. Has he ever seen or heard of anything approaching it in his practice, in his books of practice, in tradition, or in the reports?

This most extraordinary and ridiculous order was passed 10th February, 1596–7, and was immediately carried into execution.[1] Any modern chancellor or judge who should pronounce such a despotic and high-handed sentence would be deemed insane. The practice in such cases is familiar and well settled. It simply requires the striking out, on exception or motion, of the irrelevant matter, at the cost of the responsible party, and, in very aggravated cases of abuse, the imposition of a reasonable fine. The merciless infliction of unnecessary personal humiliation was an act of tyranny imported from the practice, or practices, of the star chamber. The incident was designed to be, and naturally became, one of great public notoriety. We hear of no indignation aroused by the spectacle. Harsh and cruel as it was, the action of the court was probably much applauded as a vigorous effort to stamp out an enormous evil which was making the court of

[1] Preliminary proceedings leading up to this order had been pending since the 7th of May, 1595, as already seen.

chancery a reproach. This practical joke of the chancellor at the scrivener's expense was on the popular side. The incident was perfectly fresh when Falstaff appeared upon the stage. A more vivid, fantastic, and picturesque illustration of "equity stirring" cannot well be imagined than this mirth-provoking scene. The grim humor of it jumped exactly with the coarse and cruel sport of that bear-baiting age. To an Elizabethan audience the allusion was immensely comical; and Falstaff's swearing by "*no equity stirring*" was all the more irresistibly ludicrous at the recollection of the farcical plight of the unhappy scrivener dragged around Westminster Hall from court to court with his bare head stuck through a hole in his own preposterous parchment.

These two explanations are consistent with each other, and their effect is cumulative. Whether we assume, with Halliwell-Phillipps, that the First Part of *Henry IV.* was publicly represented for the first time in the spring of 1597, or assume with Mr. Stokes that it was not exhibited until the close of that year, the result is practically the same.[1] The chancellor's order in the case of the unlucky scrivener was passed, as we have seen, on the 10th of February, 1597, and the chancellor's order referring the case of Throckmorton *v.* Finch to the twelve judges, in

[1] Outlines, i. 153; Sto. Chron. Order, 54.

obedience to the royal mandate, was passed 28th of May, 1597. But Throckmorton's bill and Finch's demurrer, the chancellor's opinion in favor of Throckmorton, and Coke's appeal to the queen to interfere, had all taken place prior to the last-named date. Here were two contemporaneous cases of great publicity conspiring with each other to bring the court of chancery and its proceedings into unusual prominence, as the "observed of all observers." Essentially differing in their facts, and differing in their principles, these two cases united in deepening the impression that the court of chancery was not a slumbering volcano, but in a state of active eruption. The combined impression made by these two cases was calculated to penetrate through every stratum of society, from the highest to the lowest. If the intelligent and thoughtful classes were more concerned with the grave historic issue involved in the fresh outbreak of the "war between the courts," the roughly facetious horseplay of the chancellor and the scrivener was a screaming farce for the groundlings, the attorneys' clerks and the leather-jerkined apprentices. It has already been seen that at the same precise time the playwright himself, as a business man, and for business purposes, had his own attention fixed upon the court of chancery, where an important case was pending in which he had a family and personal interest, and which he was backing, as will be shown hereafter, to the full extent of his means.

The very natural inquiry remains to be answered, Why has this last-mentioned explanation also escaped the attention of the learned commentators?

It may be recalled that the silence of the commentators with regard to the explanation previously offered was attributed to a common error, typically represented by a misleading statement of dates in Blackstone's Commentaries. For their being thrown off the scent in the present instance, an error of an old chancery reporter, worse and more dangerous than Blackstone's, because more obscure and difficult of detection, may possibly be held responsible.

It unfortunately happened that, outside of the original record remaining in MSS. in the registrar's custody, the only chancery reporter who professed to report the case of Mylward *v.* Weldon was a very inaccurate one named Tothill. When Aaron Burr was a practising lawyer in New York, he cited a case from Tothill's reports in argument before Chancellor Kent. Chancellor Kent condemned the book as "unfit to serve as a guide and unworthy to be cited as authority."[1]

In undertaking, many years after the event, to report this case of Mylward *v.* Weldon, the

[1] King *v.* Baldwin, 2 John. Ch. 558, 9.

author referred to, with his usual inaccuracy, assigned a wrong date to the notable order of the chancellor. In point of fact, he was so wide of the mark as to refer it to the eighth year of Elizabeth.[1]

This was some *thirty years earlier than the actual date*, which, as has been seen, corresponded practically with Falstaff's first appearance upon the stage.

This error remained undetected during the whole period of the early commentators — that is to say, during the time when the ruts were being worn which have been mainly followed since. And so the matter stood until nearly the middle of the nineteenth century, when two important works of original research appeared almost simultaneously. In November, 1845, Lord Campbell published his "Lives of the Chancellors," followed soon after by Spence's "Equitable Jurisdiction of the Court of Chancery." Each of these writers independently, the one ignoring, the other exposing the blunder of Tothill, took the trouble to search the original record in Mylward *v.* Weldon,[2] and each of them restored the correct date, as already given upon their authority.

In one respect, Lord Campbell's report of this case is more accurate than that of Mr. Spence.

[1] Tothill, Rep. 101.

[2] Reg. Liber A, 1596, folio 672.

The latter, not observing that the date of the order, "10 February, 1596," was "Old Style," attributes it to Lord Keeper Puckering. Puckering, however, died in the preceding April, and was succeeded by Sir Thomas Egerton, afterwards Lord Ellesmere, to whom Lord Campbell correctly refers the torture of the unhappy scrivener. It is true that this authentic correction has now been before the public for half a century. The simple fact appears to be, that during all that time, no one while reading the true report of this case has happened to think of Falstaff and his queer allusion to "equity stirring," and no one while enjoying Falstaff has happened to think of the equally queer order of the chancellor in Mylward *v.* Weldon. The close relation between these two distinct and apparently incongruous lines of thought is at once established by the simple recognition of their coincidence in point of time. The discovery of that relation was not likely to be made otherwise than by one of those lucky accidents which sometimes happen to a professional detective, who stumbles upon a lot of stolen bonds which have never been missed, or whose loss has been forgotten, while tracing the larceny of a watch.

Lord Campbell was a well-read Shakespearian scholar, and it is not a little remarkable that this coincidence should have escaped his notice.

His lordship tells us that he spent one of his

vacations in going through the plays and poems in search of legal allusions and terms, of which nearly one hundred had already been reported by Malone and Rushton. He succeeded in increasing the number, some of which, however, are of doubtful application, to one hundred and sixty. Falstaff's "*equity stirring*" contrived, as usual, to slip through his lordship's fingers, and is conspicuous by its absence from his lordship's list.[1]

Upon this side of the Atlantic, great learning and industry have been devoted to the same investigation by an admirable group of scholars. None of them, in their eager quest, have recognized in Falstaff's "equity" a term of the slightest juridical significance.

One of the ablest, indeed, of the American critics referred to, went so far as to hazard the assertion that no allusion to the court of chancery could be found in the whole of Shakespeare's writings, "not a single phrase or word, much less any application of any principle, peculiar to the chancery."[2]

Clear contemporaneous evidence of reported cases shows, beyond a reasonable doubt, that here we have a phrase peculiar to the chancery, with at least two distinct and pointed applications, one to its principles, the other to its procedure. It

1 Campbell's Legal Acquirements of Shakespeare.

2 Davis's Law in Shakespeare, 43, 117.

remains to be seen from the documents of still another case, in connection with surrounding circumstances, whether the same prolific stock does not bear even a third branch of application to the chancery, involving both its principles and procedure.

If all that be true, or even probably true, or the half of it, it follows at least that no future editors of Shakespeare can afford to maintain the exhaustive silence of preceding commentators. Their motto must be, when they come to the Gadshill highway-robbery act,

> "wherein fat Falstaff
> Hath a great scene ; *the image of the jest*
> *I 'll show you here at large.*"[1]

[1] *Merry Wives of Windsor*, Act IV. scene 6.

CHAPTER XII

REVIEW AND RESTATEMENT

The results summed up as to the twofold application to the chancery. — A third application suggested of a more personal character.

In the vast field of Shakespearian literature scarcely a fence corner is now to be found untilled. With a single exception, no character, and, without exception, no comic character, has been more exhaustively exploited than Falstaff. In that part of the field especially, an uncleared patch, a spot of native wilderness, would scarcely be looked for. And yet, in the words so often quoted, we find an expression of Falstaff that has for some reason been absolutely avoided or neglected. For several years the challenge has been before the public to produce a single allusion to this passage in print, other than the passing observation of Mr. Donnelly: "The language is forced; this is not a natural expression."[1] Although coming from a distinguished source, this criticism, except in these pages, remains unanswered.

[1] Great Cryptogram, 524.

Their aim and object is to show that the expression quoted was and is one of the most spontaneous and natural of all Falstaff's sayings, and that none of his good points was in its day more quickly taken nor more heartily relished. Rich with contemporaneous meaning, it is in fact a typical illustration of Falstaff's humor at its best.

There has been, and there will be, in these pages, no "conjectural emendation," no reading of anything into or out of the text, no far-fetched inferences from speculative premises, and no "æsthetic criticism." The dates and data relied on are all furnished by authentic record evidence. Certain things have been and will be assumed. Shakespeare wrote for stage effect rather than the closet. This is especially true of his comedies.[1] He was always alert for a *double-entendre*, an *equivoque*, a quirk, or a quibble. He was pretty sure upon occasion to bring in a local side allusion, or what we should now call a "gag." Above all, the expert use of professional legal terminology was to him "familiar as his garter."[2] Falstaff was his typical comic character, and the success of Falstaff was electric.

[1] "On sait bien que les comédies ne sont faites que pour être jouées, et je ne conseille de lire celle-ci qu'aux personnes qui ont des yeux pour découvrir, dans la lecture, tout le jeu du théâtre." (Molière, L'Amour Médecin. Au Lecteur.)

[2] This statement must be taken "subject to exceptions," exhaustively collected by Judge Allen in a recent work of original research, Notes on the Bacon-Shakespeare Question. None of these apply to the case in point.

The Gadshill incident was of all Falstaff's situations the most obstreperous and mirth-provoking. Falstaff's "*no equity stirring*" caps the climax of the Gadshill scene while the whirlwind of fun is at its fury. Of all points, that is the point where we should least expect Shakespeare's wing to weaken or Falstaff's wit to falter. On the contrary, that is just the point to look for something especially Shakespearian — something below the surface, something to illustrate the Shakespearian parable that "a jest's prosperity lies in the ear of him that hears it."

These things being assumed, either expressly or tacitly, the word "equity" has been found used by Shakespeare in three other plays in three distinct senses: 1st, in the Bible sense of "justice" (*2 Henry VI.* Act III. scene 1); 2d, in the technical sense of juridical or court equity (*Lear*, Act III. scene 6); 3d, in the still more narrow and special professional sense of a particular equitable right or claim (*K. John*, Act II. scene 1).[1]

One of these, and only one, being the sense in which the expression "*no equity stirring*" appears to have been heretofore accepted (*no justice going*), the effort thus far has been to show from contemporaneous history, hitherto overlooked in this connection (the word "history" being understood as original material for history,

[1] *Ante*, chapter ii.

in the shape of judicial records), that there was, underlying this primary or surface meaning, a distinct local side allusion to the great warfare then stirring between the courts of common law on the one side, representing a popular jealousy of the growing power of the chancellor, and the court of chancery on the other, supported by the regal authority. The issue being sharply made upon the jurisdiction of equity to interfere by injunction with common law proceedings, especially after judgment, reported cases were cited to establish the fact that the war was in progress for many years prior to the appearance of Falstaff and conspicuously flagrant at that very time.

Coupled with the side allusion to what Lord Bacon calls "this business of the chancery," there was also a gag at a ludicrous scene then recently enacted publicly in Westminster Hall under a very queer and questionable order of the lord chancellor.[1] The silence of the commentators as to both these explanations was attributed, in the case of one, to a common error as to dates represented by a misleading statement in Blackstone's Commentaries, and, in the case of the other, to a blunder of an old chancery reporter. In the former instance, the error was found to be one not uncommon in historical treatment, where, by an illusion of perspective, events become foreshortened and dates distorted.

[1] *Ante*, chapter xi.

"Shakespeare is not to be judged by ordinary rules,"[1] and in the case of any other author the attempt to extract still another and distinct meaning from this already highly charged expression would seem extravagant. If this author had a mental habit developed to an excessive degree it was the passion for word-play. "Fine of his fines . . . to have his fine pate full of fine dirt."[2] The scholar would lose all patience to see this point amplified by a string of such illustrations. If, upon approved principles of interpretation, any expression of Shakespeare is found fairly susceptible of a particular meaning, it is no reason for rejecting that meaning that the same expression has also been found susceptible of other and distinct significations, not necessarily repugnant.

With profound insight, it has been observed by a brilliant American critic, that there are passages where, to carry out some conception to "the finest lines and features of the thought, to push some conceit to the remotest extravagance, so that it is necessary for a well-read lawyer to make special investigation into the laws and statutes of that time before he can follow it, Shakespeare exhausts the capacity of the terms he employs."[3]

The two explanations just suggested are non-

[1] Outlines, ii. 332.

[2] *Hamlet*, Act V. scene 1. "Nul homme n'a soumis les mots à une pareille torture." (Taine.)

[3] Davis's The Law in Shakespeare, 49.

committal with respect to the question of authorship. For all the purposes of those explanations, Bacon might as well have written the play as Shakespeare. The juridical sense attributed to the word "equity" in nowise tends to impugn the theory that the author of the play must have been a jurist. It is with some diffidence that a controversial topic has now to be approached, bristling with opposition. The conception that this word "equity" was at the same time used in the professional sense of a particular equitable right or claim,[1] and with a personal allusion to a pending chancery suit in which the man of Stratford was himself deeply interested,[2] is one which all believers in the Baconian authorship are naturally inclined to repudiate *ex officio*. From them especially I bespeak a patient hearing of what they will at least find to be no rehash of stale controversy, but the result, such as it is, of original research in a comparatively unexplored field. No overt attempt will be made to attack with argument their favorite theory, for the fact of the Shakespearian authorship will be frankly assumed throughout.[3]

[1] As used in *K. John*, Act II. scene 1.

[2] Shakespeare *v.* Lambert.

[3] Some may object to this language as treating the Bacon heresy with too much respect. At the time these words were written, in 1892, the delusion was still held by many respectable people who have since had their eyes opened by a more thorough investigation. The views advanced herein, bearing on the Lam-

bert litigation, may have contributed in some small measure to this result. The personal application of "equity stirring" to that litigation was not denied by Mr. Donnelly himself, in a characteristic letter to the writer, in which he claims to have discovered a great number of occult references to this litigation in several plays, and endeavors to make them consistent with his favorite theory, by *assuming that Bacon must have been counsel for the Shakespeares.* It is needless to say that for this assumption there is no foundation.

CHAPTER XIII

LITTLE WILL SHAXBERE

Looks out upon a world of litigation. — Stratford court. — John Shakespeare, bailiff and judge. — His son's law school.

WHILE the First Part of *Henry IV.* was in course of preparation for the stage, and while the war between the courts was in progress, in the manner already attempted to be shown, there was likewise war between the house of Shakespeare and the house of Lambert. Before going into the particulars of this long and bitter family litigation, first in the court of queen's bench, and afterwards in two suits in the court of chancery, it will be necessary to look into the elaborate and costly scheme of conveyancing to effect the mortgage upon mother Shakespeare's property to Edmund Lambert, her brother-in-law, the alleged legal forfeiture of which, affirmed on the one side and denied on the other, was the *casus belli.*

Now, as all this is matter of supreme insignificance to us, except so far as it may enter into the life of William Shakespeare and possibly leave its stamp upon his pages, let the effort be to view the whole transaction from his standpoint, and, so far as possible, with his eyes. In order to do this, we must first attempt to get at least a partial view of the general environment.[1]

The age of Elizabeth, distinguished in many respects, was emphatically an age of litigation. The queen was herself a frequent and fierce litigant. The royal taste for sport was, in her case, indulged by hunting down human game through the brakes and thickets of the law. The pronounced effect upon the methods of conveyancing of a recent statute[2] involved the raising and adjudication of a multitude of new questions pertaining to the law of real estate. The extension of commerce, the development of manufactures, the growing importance of personal property, the multiplication of contracts, swelled the dockets with a new order of business. Along with this came a marked increase in the number of damage suits, slander cases taking the lead. The voluminous law reports of the period[3] give but an inadequate idea of the general prevalence and activity

[1] "Pour avoir la vérité, il faut se placer au point de vue de l'époque." (Renan, Etudes, 142.)

[2] Stat. of Uses, 27 Henry VIII. cap. 10; Alexander's Brit. St. in Force in Maryland, 292.

[3] Plowden, Coke, Croke, Popham, Anderson, Owen, Yelverton, Leonard, Moore, etc. The reports of this reign contain more questions upon personal rights and contracts than those of all previous reigns together. The tendency to bring actions upon the most trivial causes attracted the notice of Parliament, and statutes were passed to check it. (3 Reeves, Hist. C. Law, 678, 764.)

of litigation. Those reports are mainly occupied with the proceedings of the superior courts at Westminster Hall. But, in addition to these, there existed a multitude of inferior local tribunals throughout the realm, whose proceedings are not reported, although technically courts of record. Almost every petty borough had its "court of record," bringing "justice," as the thing was politely called, "home to every man's door."

Some of these local courts existed by prescription or ancient custom, like the court of the mayor and sheriff of London at Guildhall.[1] Others were chartered by Act of Parliament. Still another class, of which the Stratford court was an example, was established by royal letters-patent.[2] Their terms were frequent and short, usually twice a month. Their jurisdiction was concurrent, with some exceptions, with the civil jurisdiction of the superior courts of common law, to whose superintendence they were subject.[3] Their procedure was assimilated to the practice of the superior courts, except that cases were not commenced by original writ, but by "plaint."[4] The forms in use were sufficiently technical and arbitrary to afford ample opportunity for chicane.

[1] 9 Rep. 62, 69; Smith *v.* Hillier, Cro. Eliz. 167, 168; 1 Leon. 52.

[2] Shackspeare *v.* Addenbrooke, Outlines, ii. 79, par. VII.

[3] 3 Bl. Com. 81, 272.

[4] Framson *v.* Delamere, Cro. Eliz. 458; 1 Leon. 132, 185.

All the pleadings were required to be in law Latin, a mongrel jargon which would have made Cicero and all Rome howl.[1] This rule was strictly enforced, and the superior courts especially enjoyed reversing their judgments when the proceedings were in good English instead of bad Latin.[2] Of course, attorneys were necessary to conduct the business of these petty courts. Stratford had half-a-dozen or more, and appears to have had "counselors" also.[3] The presiding judge was the mayor of the corporation, or an equivalent functionary called the bailiff, or high bailiff.[4] The ministerial officer to execute process was the sergeant-at-mace.[5] The important officer who was relied upon to help out the judge for the time being with his Latin and his law was the clerk or steward. A case is reported where the title to one of these offices was a subject of litigation.[6] Issues of fact were tried by jury; and in short, these petty tribunals imitated the paraphernalia and pomp of the courts of Westminster Hall.

It is a significant fact, not hitherto sufficiently appreciated, that when the eyes of William Shake-

[1] See specimens in Outlines, ii. 78–80, 215, etc.; also, in Appendix C.

[2] Lucas *v.* Donne, Cro. Eliz. 185.

[3] Outlines, ii. 215.

[4] Smith *v.* Hillier, Cro. Eliz. 167; Outlines, ii. 230.

[5] *Serviens ad clavam*, Barkly *v.* Kempstow, Cro. Eliz. 123; 9 Rep. 62, 69; Outlines, ii. 77, 224, 230, 238.

[6] Case of the clerk and steward of the court of pleas in Peterborough, Lacy *v.* Whetston, Cro. Eliz. 343.

speare first looked forth upon the outer world, they saw it through the medium of an atmosphere of litigation. Not long after the removal of his father, John Shakespeare, to Stratford-on-Avon (about 1551) the inhabitants of that borough were made happy by the establishment there of their new "court of record."[1] They had already their "court leet" of petty criminal jurisdiction, and in this court John Shakespeare appears to have had his first taste of law by being fined twelvepence for maintaining what was classically called a *sterquinarium* in front of his house on Henly Street.[2] This was in 1552, and soon after we find him fairly started upon a long career of almost constant litigation, varied by frequent service as a juror and by occasional service as an affeeror or assessor of fines (in the court leet) and as referee or arbitrator. The register of the Stratford court of record is unfortunately imperfect,[3] but from that part of it which is extant it is interesting to note that from 1556 to 1601 John Shakespeare was actively connected with some forty odd lawsuits, most of them in the Stratford court of record, and most of them cases for small amounts, in which he figured either as plaintiff or defendant.[4] This enumeration, it will

[1] By virtue of letters-patent of Edward VI. in 1553. (Wheler, Hist. and Antiq. of Stratford-upon-Avon.)

[2] Outlines, ii. 215.

[3] Outlines, ii. 77.

[4] Outlines, ii. 215, etc.

be observed, is only a partial one, and does not of course include cases the minutes of which are lost, nor the still more numerous line of cases in which he served as juror or presided as judge.

Local politics as well as practical law were among the incidental occupations of Shakespeare's father. During all this time he was climbing the ladder of municipal preferment and passing through the borough offices; from chamberlain in 1561 to alderman in 1565; to high bailiff in 1568; to chief alderman in 1571; and in 1572 he was appointed a sort of local dictator, the object of which extraordinary commission does not appear.[1]

"Little pitchers have big ears." We do not read in any book, except the book of nature, that the eager ears of little "*Will Shaxbere*" (so spelt by the Stratford schoolmaster), then well advanced in his fifth year, shrewdly took in the animated talk at the family table over his father's promotion to the judicial dignity of high bailiff.[2]

[1] Outlines, ii. 232.

[2] In a familiar letter from Lincoln to an intimate friend, Oct. 22, 1846, he writes of his son "Bob": "He is quite smart enough. I sometimes fear he is one of the little rare-ripe sort that are smarter at about five than ever after." (Lamon's Life of L. 278.) For the benefit of those who require the evidence of printed books, a few random illustrations are added of the development of personal characteristics at or about the age mentioned. Plutarch records a remarkable instance of heroism in Cato (Uticensis) when that young gentleman was under five years of age. Grotius made fair Latin verses, Mozart composed

Mary Arden Shakespeare was naturally proud of her husband's advancement, and none the less so

minuets, and Bentham had taken a course of history, and was reading Latin and French, at the same age. Detaille says of himself, "My first visit to England was when I was only five years of age, and I spoiled our passport by drawing little pictures all over it." Renan tells us that at the age of six he announced his purpose to become an author. (Souvenirs, 146.) Boughton tells us that he used to draw "elephants, sailors, and wild Indians pretty well, and not childishly, when only five." (Strand Mag. xx. 4.) Indeed, Michael Angelo began to draw "as soon as he could use his hands." (Grimm, i. 40.) The Dauphin had just passed his fifth year when his smart replies elicited from Lafayette the remark, "There are no more children." (St. Amand.) Paul Dombey was nearly five when he puzzled his father with the series of questions beginning, "Papa, what 's money?" "The age of prying curiosity is from four and a half to nine." (Charles O'Malley, ii. 375.) Browning wrote an imitation of Ossian when less than five years old, to which Miss Barrett replies that she "used to make rhymes over her bread and milk when nearly a baby." (Letters, i. 400, 403; ii. 467.) Kingsley before his fifth year preached sermons and wrote verses which may be seen in print. (Letters and Life of Kingsley, ch. i.)

"Mrs. Hannah More was fond of relating how she called at Mr. Macaulay's, and was met by a fair, pretty, slight child, with abundance of light hair, about four years of age, who came to the front door to tell her that his parents were out, but that if she would be good enough to come in he would bring her a glass of old spirits; a proposition which greatly startled the old lady, who had never aspired beyond cowslip wine. When questioned as to what he knew about old spirits he could only say that Robinson Crusoe often had some."

It was not very long after that incident that the learned child with the phenomenal memory began a compendium of universal history, giving a tolerably connected view of the leading events from the creation down, filling about a quire of paper. (Trevelyan's Life of Lord Macaulay, ch. i.)

Other instances will readily occur to the scholar, and in fact they might be extended indefinitely.

because her own means and family connection had been factors in the result. John Shakespeare may or may not have been able to write,[1] but there is no evidence that he was dumb. The prying curiosity of their oldest son, stimulated by their conversation, was far from satisfied by their smiling answers to his persevering inquiries. He wanted to witness with his own inquisitive eyes the spectacle of his father actually presiding in a court of justice, and we may be sure that a bright morning came, when his father made an era in his young life by taking his little hand, and leading the future dramatist to the drama of real life, as enacted in a court-room.

There he would be tickled by the flattering notice taken of the judge's son. He would be excited by the throng, interested by the variety of feature and costume, astonished by the bawling of the crier, impressed by the kissing of the book by the jurors and witnesses, amused by the testimony of the Stratford clowns, delighted by the sharp cross-examinations, the wrangling of the lawyers, and the laughter of the crowd. The important airs assumed by the sergeant-at-mace, with his conspicuous badge of office, would not escape his notice. By repeated visits he would become familiar with the scene. His attention would be attracted by the bustling manner of

[1] There appears to be a schism upon this question among experts.

some officious attorney, and he would notice, with Chaucer, that, after all, he ever "seemed busier than he was," and with Molière, that he, "sans aucune affaire, est toujours affairé." Above all, he would with honest pride recognize upon the august elevation of the bench the familiar form of his father, posing now as

> "the justice,
> In fair round belly, with good capon lined,
> With eyes severe, and beard of formal cut,
> Full of wise saws and modern instances,"[1]

an ample stock of these last being the garnered fruitage of a long and somewhat costly personal experience.

In all this there would be much that the precocious, quick-witted child could not at first understand, and that almost any other child would not care to understand. The faculty in which genius begins to differentiate from mediocrity is the faculty of observation. When mediocrity comes to something it does not understand, it looks the difficulty blandly in the face and passes on to something else. Genius looks at it again and again, walks around it, gets behind it, finds something to compare with it, picks it to pieces, puts it together, and in the end appropriates it.

There is no reason to assume that such a boy as Shakespeare must have been, to be the "father

[1] *As You Like It*, Act II. scene 7.

of the man," would have failed to use his tongue and his ears as well as his eyes, or that by dint of pertinacious questioning he did not gradually succeed in extracting from his father so much as his father was able to tell him, and that was considerable, of the real meaning of all those "wise saws and modern instances," the legal forms and terms of art he so often heard repeated. For the rest, he had free access to the steward or clerk of the court and the practicing attorneys, and doubtless their good-will. Not one of these functionaries but would take a lively interest in the smart son of the high bailiff. Oftentimes, when tired of playing hockey, tennis, or nine men's morris, we may imagine the destined actor and playwright resorting to the realistic comedy which was always on tap at the Guildhall, admission free, and getting there just the sort of amusement and instruction that his nature craved. It was a school of human nature as well as a school of law. It probably suited his taste much better than the Accidence and the Sententiæ Pueriles which are supposed to have been the sources of the "little Latin" he learned at the Stratford free school.[1]

> "All the learnings that his time
> Could make him the receiver of, he took
> As we do air, fast as 't was ministered;
> And in his spring became a harvest."[2]

[1] Outlines, i. 53.

[2] *Cymbeline*, Act I. scene 1.

As already stated, no printed book can be quoted for these glimpses into Shakespeare's child-life, and every student will take them for what he may think them to be worth upon his own estimate of probabilities. Given the Stratford court of record; given John Shakespeare the chronic litigant, occasional referee, standing juror, and finally judge; given the pages of William Shakespeare stamped all over with idiomatic law, and not a particle of direct proof that he was ever an attorney or an attorney's clerk,—and we have a pressing presumption that in the Stratford court of record he found the rudiments of such limited legal education as he had.

The practical education of the youthful poet by his father and his father's court may be called *Shakespeare's elementary law school.* It may be that the course was superficial and desultory, but it was sufficient to initiate him into much of the *technique* of the profession, and to familiarize him with the legal images, the terms and conceits which so richly stud the plays and poems. And this was by no means the whole of his professional training. As will be seen a little farther on, when we come to the Gibbs lease and the Lambert mortgage, he was to experience another course in the school of the conveyancer and the learning of fines, and still another in the management of lawsuits between his parents and John Lambert, upon both sides of Westminster Hall.

CHAPTER XIV

HIS SCHOOL OF INSANITY

Lunatics confined in jails. — Bailiffs of corporations keepers of jails. — Shakespeare's familiarity with alienism. — Exceptional opportunity for studies in insanity.

Before passing from the subject of John Shakespeare, bailiff and judge of the Stratford court, and the influence of that circumstance in shaping the mental tendencies of his eldest son, there is one point which has never been noted, too interesting and suggestive to be passed without incidental mention, because tending to account for the great dramatist's extraordinary familiarity with all the types and phases of insanity.

The fact is well known, that in his day there were no adequate hospitals for insane patients, who were, when at all troublesome, confined in the nearest jail.[1]

It appears from reported cases of the period that it was not considered at all incompatible with the dignity of mayor or bailiff and judge of

[1] "*Tranio:* Call forth an officer. [Enter one with an officer.] Carry this mad knave to the jail." (*Taming of the Shrew*, Act V. scene 1.)

a municipal corporation, such as that of John Shakespeare of the borough of Stratford, to hold at the same time the humble office of jailer. In fact, it is expressly stated by Coke in one of the cases referred to, that such was "the course of *all corporations*," adding, that it is "incident to a court to have a jail," and that "a jail is not a place certain, but goeth with the person of the jailer."[1]

It further appears that this was a function, like that of "sutler to the camp," from which "profits" did "accrue." The bailiff, as common jailer, had the boarding of his prisoners at the public expense. Superfluous prisoners were boarded out, and responsible persons could be found willing to undertake the safe-keeping of presumably eligible inmates, under the flattering inducement of thereby making their "commodity" by "uttering meat and drink."[2]

It is easy to see that privileged persons, having access to jails in those times, would enjoy special advantages for observation of cases of mental alienation; in other words, for studies in insanity.

Now, there is no direct written evidence that bailiff Shakespeare's eldest son ever showed the slightest interest in his father's jail, or ever once gratified a boyish curiosity by taking a peep at the queer cases it contained.

[1] Smith *v.* Hillier, Cro. Eliz. 167, 8.

[2] Barkly *v.* Kempstow, Cro. Eliz. 123.

But, all the same, is not the fact plainly written in the book of nature? And is not the evidence of the book of nature plainly confirmed in the lines of *Lear* and *Hamlet?*

Neither is there a shred of direct written evidence that harmless cases of mental alienation — idiots, fools, or cranks — were at any time lodged in that particular bailiff's house and boarded at his table, or that John Shakespeare made his "commodity" by "uttering meat and drink" to such cases, at the expense of the borough.

All we have here is a general presumption from a prevalent custom, the custom itself being fully in evidence. Coupled with that presumption, we have the phenomenon of an extensive and exact psychological knowledge, so remarkable in fact that the conclusion is irresistible that "abnormal conditions of mind had attracted Shakespeare's diligent observation, and had been his favorite study."[1]

Whatever the books may not have to say upon the subject, it is impossible for the coldest nature not to kindle at the thought that here we may have in our hands the clue which leads directly to the very source of those early, fresh, and vivid impressions of insanity that later matured into the ripe experiences of the accomplished alienist.

At Stratford-upon-Avon, a short distance from

[1] The Mad Folk of Shakespeare, by John Charles Bucknill, M. D., London.

the "Birthplace," the visitor is still shown what is called the "Cage," a gloomy vaulted cellar under the house where Shakespeare's daughter Judith afterwards lived with her husband, Thomas Quiney. Tradition makes this "Cage" the dungeon for incorrigibles when the house was used as the borough prison. If so used, as is supposed, at the time John Shakespeare was bailiff of Stratford, the prison under his charge was within a couple of minutes' walk of his residence. It is by no means a likely supposition that the destined actor and dramatist was kept in ignorance of this prison, so near his home, of its purposes, or of its inmates, or that his access to it was made either impossible or difficult, either during the period of his father's official connection with it or afterwards.

Of course, it cannot be claimed that the fact is established beyond all controversy. Every scholar knows that within the nebulous sphere Shakespearian, anything like dogmatism is as absurd as the affectation of infallibility. The most that can be claimed for the idea is that it is not a mere gratuitous speculation, and that appears to rest upon a rational basis of probability, supported by authentic record evidence.

What lends it importance and vests it with fascinating interest is that it nearly concerns the very highest intellectual attribute of the world's greatest dramatic poet.

The revelation, if it be one, came of itself, without being looked for, expected, or suspected. It came by the simple process of relation, the putting together of two concurrent facts, — the fact that lunatics were confined in jail, and the fact (presumed from a general usage) that Shakespeare's father kept a jail at the time when the boy's mind had reached the awakening and inquisitive stage.

The cautious inquirer will doubtless require direct and positive proof of additional details. He will ask for evidence that the usage of "all corporations" specially applied to the corporation of Stratford;[1] evidence that bailiff Shakespeare, even if he did keep a jail, ever had charge of a single madman or madwoman; evidence that if he had insane persons under his charge, his little five-year-old boy ever took the slightest notice of them; evidence that if the child ever did take notice of them, it was anything more than the cursory notice which all children take of all sorts of queer things within their range of vision.

These are the missing links, to supply which requires a high appreciation of the dramatist's mastery of the phenomena of mental disturbance, of his exceptional powers of observation and

[1] Such limited examination of the borough accounts and archives at the "Birthplace" as the writer was able to make, with the indispensable aid of the obliging librarian, Mr. Richard Savage (in August, 1900), failed to disclose any conclusive indications, either affirmative or negative.

assimilation, and of the necessity for supposing that these exceptional powers had, at some time and in some way, exceptional opportunities for cultivation. These exceptional opportunities are supplied upon the hypothesis now advanced. No other explanation has ever been offered.

In the learned work already cited, Dr. Bucknill gives the conventional or commonly received opinion upon this subject, as follows: "There is no reason to suppose that when Shakespeare wrote, any other asylum for the insane existed in this country than the then poor and small establishment of Bethlem Hospital (Bedlam). In his time the insane were not secluded from the world as they are now. If their symptoms were prominent and dangerous they were indeed thrust out of sight very harshly and effectually; but if their liberty was in any degree tolerable, it was tolerated, and they were permitted to live in the family circle or to wander the country. Thus every one must have been brought into contact with examples of mental derangement, and any one who sought the knowledge of their peculiarities would find it at every turn."[1]

This is well put, and, with some slight exaggeration at the close, undoubtedly true. It may be added, however, that if the accomplished author's attention had been called to the custom prevalent in the sixteenth century, the custom of

[1] The Mad Folk of Shakespeare, 10.

"all corporations" as stated by Coke, that the mayor or bailiff acted *ex officio* as the borough jailer, it is not at all likely that the competent expert quoted would have failed to notice the fact that, from the special opportunities thus presented, the Stratford bailiff's eldest son was much more highly privileged than the casual wayfarer for studies in the school of insanity.

The cases referred to as showing the custom for the head officer of the borough corporation, whether called bailiff or mayor, to act also as keeper of the prison and of the prisoners will be found extracted below.

Cro. El. 123–4.

BARKLY AND GIBBS *against* KEMPSTOW.

Trinity Term, 30 Elizabeth.

Assumpsit: Plaintiffs declare, that *civitas Worcester fuit antiqua civitas*, and that all pleas determinable there were used to be by suit before the bailiffs, chamberlain, and aldermen there determined, and the bailiffs, etc., had use to have their *servientem ad clavam*, to make arrests ; and that there they had a prison, and that the bailiffs time out of mind were keepers of the prison, and of all the prisoners there; and that whereas the defendant had a house adjoining to the prison, in which the bailiffs had use to commit their prisoners to be safely kept; and whereas one M. had affirmed a plaint of 18*l.* against Worsley in the same court before the bailiff, etc., which was a plea there determinable by custom, *per quod* they *mandaverunt quoddam warrantum* to the said sergeant to arrest him, by force whereof he arrested him and brought him to the next court, and the plaintiffs being bailiffs committed him to prison; and the defendant having the said house adjoining to the prison, in consideration that the plaintiffs committed the prisoner to him to keep, by which he might make his commodity, by uttering his meat and drink, and might have as great benefit as he used to have, promised to keep him safely, and save the plaintiffs harmless of all escapes; whereupon they committed the prisoner to his house to keep, etc., he such a day suffered him to escape, by which they were damnified. Upon *non assumpsit* pleaded, it was found for the plaintiffs, and divers matters alleged in arrest of judgment. 1. Because it is alleged that *mandaverunt warrantum*, etc., but shew not that it was in writing under seal, as it ought to be. *Sed non allocatur*, for it shall be so intended. 2. It was not alleged how they were damnified, viz. that they were sued for this escape, or otherwise molested. *Sed non allocatur*, for immediately upon the escape they were damnified and in danger to be sued, and might sue the defendant presently, and not tarry till they were sued.

It was held upon good advisement, that this was a good consideration to make an *assumpsit*, viz. the uttering of his meat, etc.

Cro. El. 167–8.

SMITH *against* HILLIER AND CLERKE.

Trinity Term, 31 Elizabeth.

False Imprisonment: in Middlesex. The defendant pleads that *Lynn* is an ancient village, and that in it *usitatum est a tempore quo*, etc., to chuse a mayor every year, and that the mayor for all the time, etc., was *custos gaolæ* there; and shewed, that a plaint was entered in the court there against the plaintiff, for which he was committed by the mayor to the gaol there, *absque hoc* that they are guilty of the imprisonment in *Middlesex;* upon which the plaintiff demurs.

Tanfield for the plaintiff. The bar is not good. First. Because the prescription is, that for all the time, etc., the mayors had been keepers of the gaol, which was no good pleading of the custom; for he ought to say *usitatum est*, etc. Secondly. The mayor cannot commit one to himself, for there ought to be one to commit, and another to receive; and not to be both one person. Thirdly. He doth not prescribe to have a gaol there, nor sheweth not there was a gaol there; and it may be, that he may make his gaol where he pleaseth, and then the plea should be *commissus custodiæ majoris*, and not to the gaol; or the prescription should be, that the mayor, etc., was *custos* of all prisoners, and not *custos gaolæ*.

Coke for the defendants. The bar is good, notwithstanding

the exceptions. First. It is once alleged, that *usitatum est* to chuse a mayor, etc., then *usitatum est* shall be referred to every part of the prescription, and need not reiterate it to every part. Secondly. The course of all corporations is, that the mayor which is the judge, is gaoler also: so the sheriffs of *London*, they have a court in the *Guildhall*, and are officers and gaolers to it. Thirdly. He need not prescribe in the gaol; for it is incident for a court to have a gaol, as a court of piepowders to a fair; also a gaol is not in a place certain, but goeth with the person of the gaoler.

And of the same opinion was The Court, *in omnibus:* and it was adjudged for the defendants.

CHAPTER XV

ORIGIN OF THE LAMBERT WAR

Asbies estate. — Gibbs lease. — Mortgage to Lambert. — Lambert claims forfeiture. — John Shakespeare claims a tender.

THESE glimpses extend over a period of some ten years. The boy has entered his fifteenth year. His joyous childhood has ended, and he finds himself called on to face a stormy future. His father's "happy hours are done and past, and his estate shrinks from him."[1] Whether from excess of hospitality to keep up his municipal state, or from business misfortunes, in 1578 John Shakespeare finds himself with a large family on his hands, "heinously unprovided." The question of ways and means becomes the great subject of household discussion. To obtain temporary relief from pressing claims the sum of forty pounds must be had at once. Years ago, in California, when an adventurer disappeared, the stereotyped answer to inquiries was: "Gone back to his wife's relations." Edmund Lambert, of Barton-on-the-Heath, was the husband of Mrs.

[1] *Timon of Athens*, Act III. scene 2.

Shakespeare's sister Joan, and was willing to lend forty pounds upon the security of a small landed property which Mrs. Shakespeare held under her father's will. William Shakespeare had been withdrawn from school to assist his father in business. There is no direct evidence that he was a party to the family consultations in the matter of the Lambert mortgage, but from the nature of the case it is highly probable that he knew all about it from the first, and that such services as he was able to render in its furtherance, by carrying messages and otherwise, were called into requisition.[1] However that may be, it is certain that at a later stage of the transaction he was brought in as a party in a manner to be explained farther on.

The property in question consisted of a house with nearly sixty acres of land, known as Asbies. It was situated in the parish of Aston-Cantlow, in the hamlet of Wilmecote, about three miles from Stratford. The property, with the exception of the house, had but recently been made the subject of a somewhat complicated transaction, amounting to a lease for twenty-one years from Michaelmas, 1580, to one George Gibbs, at the practically nominal rent of about eight bushels of grain.[2]

[1] Compare General Grant's recollection of a business transaction of his father when Ulysses was a boy of ten. (Persl. Mem. of U. S. Grant, i. 22.)

[2] Outlines, ii. 202, where will be found a Latin copy of the fine

If there be anything in the surmise of Halliwell-Phillips that the lessee, Gibbs, was a mere trustee,[1] the door is wide open for the unpleasant suspicion that the lease was after all a scheme to protect from his creditors John Shakespeare's life interest in his wife's estate. Fraudulent devices to evade creditors were, in fact, the fashion of the day. In his report of a famous and leading case, Coke says: "*Crescit in orbe dolus.* Fraud and deceit abound in these days more than in former times."[2] Fraudulent conveyances were especially aimed at by several well-known statutes, substantially in force in this country at this day.[3] Creditors were merciless, and sometimes unscrupulous; their claims were often unjust though legal; to "fight the devil with fire" was the natural resort of the debtor

levied in the court of common pleas at Westminster to consummate the lease. It was the common practice at that time to assure a lease for a term of years by fine. (3 Reeves, Hist. Eng. Law, ch. xxx. p. 375.) The property as described calls for "70 acres of land, 6 acres of meadow, 10 acres of pasture, and common of pasture," which is considerably in excess of the Asbies holding. The discrepancy is understood when it is remembered that it was usual in fines to call for more land than was actually intended to pass. (Fermor's case, 3 Rep. 79.) For an analysis and discussion of this "double fine" and its effect as tending to explain the only known fact in Shakespeare's biography during an obscure interval of seven years, see Appendix C.

[1] Outlines, ii. 203.

[2] Twyne's case, 3 Rep. 80; 1 Smith Lead. Ca. 1.

[3] 13 Eliz. cap. v.; 27 Eliz. cap. iv.; Alex. Brit. Stat. 378, 413.

at bay. Sharp practice on the part of the creditor was thought enough to justify defensive sharp tactics by the debtor.

Among the schemes in vogue to defeat creditors, fraudulent leases were found especially handy. In Twyne's case, several precedents are cited of "leases for years by fraud and covin." Being commonly assured by fine, which was matter of record and considered the conclusive judgment of a court, they were relied on as an iron-clad protection. It was not until nearly twenty years after the Gibbs lease was made, that the courts held for the first time, and even then not without much doubt and difficulty, that a solemn fine could be vacated for fraud.[1]

There is a connecting circumstance which indicates that the Lambert mortgage was in contemplation at the time the Gibbs lease was executed. The mortgage followed close upon the lease, and by the terms of the lease it was not to commence to run until the time when the mortgage loan was made repayable (Michaelmas, 1580). The term created by the lease was limited to expire in 1601. Four years prior to that date it is referred to as still subsisting in the answer of John Lambert to the bill in chancery of Shakespeare and wife, to be hereafter mentioned, and the hope of profiting by an increased rental is charged by Lambert as

[1] Fermor's case, 3 Rep. 79.

the unjust motive of that suit. With this exception the lease in question cuts no figure in the subsequent controversy, and nothing more need be said about it further than to point out the connection in time and circumstance of the fine, which has been preserved, and of the lost indenture to lead its uses with the cumbrous conveyancing to effect the Lambert mortgage, following hard thereupon.

Compared with the ease and simplicity of similar arrangements at this day, a mortgage in those times, especially of a married woman's property, was, in the amount and variety of professional mechanism required, a thing of joy to lawyers and a nightmare to clients.[1]

On the present occasion, due compliance with

[1] Of the mortgage itself the common law conception was extremely simple, and cannot be more neatly expressed than in the exact words of Littleton, the great authority in Shakespeare's time: —

"If a feoffment be made upon such condition, that if the feoffor pay to the feoffee at a certain day, etc., £40 of money, that then the feoffor may reënter, etc., in this case the feoffee is called tenant in mortgage, which is as much to say in French as *mort gage*, and in Latin *mortuum vadium*. And it seemeth that the cause why it is called mortgage is, for that it is doubtful whether the feoffor will pay at the day limited such sum or not; and if he doth not pay, then the land which is put in pledge upon condition for the payment of the money is taken from him for ever, and so dead to him upon condition, etc. And if he doth pay the money, then the pledge is dead as to the tenant, etc." (Litt. 332.)

It will be noticed that the Lambert mortgage was to secure the typical "forty pounds" of Littleton's illustration.

all the formalities appears to have been rigidly exacted by Lambert's solicitor. There was first required an indenture of bargain and sale, under the statute of uses, next a deed of feoffment with livery of seisin at common law, and lastly the levy of a fine. Neither of the deeds is extant, but for all practical purposes they are sufficiently described in Lambert's answer in chancery.[1] The indenture bore date 14th November, 1578, and was executed by John Shakespeare alone. The consideration named was forty pounds paid by Edmund Lambert to John Shakespeare. The property is described as "one messuage and one yeard and fower acres of lande with the appurtenances, lyeinge and beinge in Wilmecott, in the parish of Aston Cawntloe, in the countie of Warwicke."[2] The grant is "to Edmunde Lamberte, his heirs and assigns forever." The condition is that the deed is to be void upon the payment by John Shakespeare to Edmund Lambert of forty pounds at Michaelmas (29th September), 1580, and the payment is to be made at the dwelling-house of the said Edmund Lambert in Barton-on-the-Heath in the county of Warwick. The deed poll with livery of seisin was also by John Shakespeare alone, "afterwards," date not given, probably the same day.

[1] Outlines, ii. 15. See Appendix B.

[2] The term *yard of land* was indefinite, and varied with the locality.

Its effect was claimed to be "to infeoff the said Edmund Lambert of the said premises to have and to hold to him and his heirs forever." This feoffment was doubtless required upon the principle then held by the bar and shortly after laid down from the bench, that "livery is of more worth and more worthy ceremony to pass estates and therefore shall be preferred to deed of bargain and sale enrolled." [1]

The two deeds had accomplished nothing more than to mortgage the life estate of John Shakespeare as "tenant by curtesy initiate." To bind the estate of the married woman, the levy of a fine was necessary, in the court of common pleas at Westminster. To achieve this formality would require expensive professional services in London. It also required the private acknowledgment of Mrs. Shakespeare, involving either a trip to London for that purpose or the issuing of a commission to Warwickshire. In any event there would be a round bill of costs.[2]

How much of the forty pounds was left to John Shakespeare after paying out of it the fees, costs, and other expenses incident to all this fine conveyancing, is a matter of pure speculation. It is hardly probable that he employed a solicitor, both from his impecunious condition and from the confidence he had in his brother-

[1] Homly *v.* Bracebridge, 1 Leon. 6.

[2] The note of the fine may be found in Appendix B.

in-law at that time. It is more likely that he looked to his son to read the papers to him (if indeed the father, as is supposed, could not write nor read writing),[1] and relied upon his own business experience for the rest.

As will be seen farther on, there is presumptive proof that young William Shakespeare was aware of every step in the transaction. If so, it was itself a fairly liberal education in real-estate law, at least for a dramatic poet. It is not by any means claimed that all the legal terms of art in the plays and poems were derived from this source. But if there should be stricken from them all the terms of art suggested by the Lambert indenture, feoffment, and fine, in connection with the Gibbs lease, there would scarcely be enough left for controversy. And yet we have not come to the actual litigation.

Edmund Lambert entered into possession of Asbies and took the rents and profits in lieu of interest, there being no provision for interest in any of the mortgage instruments. The loan became due on the 29th September (Michaelmas), 1580. It was not claimed to have been actually paid. It was claimed to have been tendered and refused.[2] A valid tender would have prevented

[1] See *ante*, page 100.

[2] The statement attributed to Edmund Lambert when he refused the forty pounds tendered was that John Shakespeare owed him other money for certain other matters which was not also tendered. (Bill in Chancery. Appendix B.)

a forfeiture as effectually as payment. But the fact of the tender was denied. Edmund Lambert held on to the property, claiming to be absolute owner by reason of the alleged forfeiture, until his death in the spring of the year 1587, when Asbies came by descent into the possession of John Lambert, his son and heir. John Shakespeare again tendered the money (as he alleged) to John Lambert and demanded possession, which was again refused. John Lambert "held the fort." [1]

[1] It will readily occur to the scholar that the word "tender" is one of Shakespeare's stock phrases. There is no word upon which the changes are more constantly rung. He puts in the mouth of Polonius a sort of apology in passing, — "not to crack the wind of the poor phrase, wronging it thus."

CHAPTER XVI

IN THE COURT OF QUEEN'S BENCH

An age of sharp practice. — Settlement attempted. — William Shakespeare a party. — Lambert repudiates. — The litigation commences in the court of queen's bench. — The law's delay. — The action at law abandoned.

THE age of Elizabeth was an age of litigation, but it was very far from being an age of law reform. Bacon was as much disgusted with the jurisprudence as with the philosophy of his time, but he found the one much harder to improve than the other. What that jurisprudence essentially lacked was the spirit of equity in its principles and in its administration. It was an age of sharp practice and of advantage-taking under the forms of law. The queen set the fashion, and gave her loyal subjects an example and an excuse for standing tenaciously upon the rigor of the law, however harsh and oppressive the result.[1] If a tenant failed to pay his rent at the

[1] We have already seen a signal illustration of this in the case of Throckmorton *v.* Finch, *supra*. The reports of the time furnish many parallels. (Borough's case, 4 Rep. 73; Bonney's case, Moore, 149; Tresham's case, Ib. 172; Knight's case, Ib. 199.) Elizabeth's cruel exaction of an old debt from one of her former

precise day, the landlord had no scruple to enforce the forfeiture. If a mortgage was in default by non-payment of the money at the very time limited, no qualm of conscience hindered the creditor from appropriating the security. If the condition of a bond was not performed to the letter, the penalty, however rigorous, was apt to be mercilessly exacted. *Under an adroitly evasive surface* the character of Shylock is, in one aspect, a vivid cartoon, broadly caricaturing this too prevalent propensity of Shakespeare's countrymen to exact, without equity and without mercy, under the name of "justice," the uttermost literal rigor of the law.[1]

favorites, Lord Chancellor Hatton, by ordering extreme legal proceedings against him, is agreed on all hands to have so affected that courtier that he died of a broken heart. (Camp. Lives Chan. ch. xlv.)

[1] Just as the much criticised verbal nibblings and quibblings of Portia to rescue the debtor Antonio from Shylock's clutches,—

> "Shed thou no blood, nor cut thou less or more,
> But just a pound of flesh," etc.
>
> (*Merchant of Venice*, Act IV. scene 1.)

were simply a burlesque, purposely made as extravagant as possible, to ridicule the pettifogging defensive devices often resorted to by counsel, and sometimes countenanced by courts. Judges in those days, while obstinately refusing to relieve the harshness of the law by admitting the principles of equity, were rather inclined to chuckle with satisfaction when they found themselves able to defeat a scheme of injustice by a cunning artifice of technicality. It may somewhat detract from their credit to be obliged to add, that, in their partiality for form over substance, it made little difference whether the claim defeated by such methods was meritorious or wickedly unjust.

What made the case particularly hard upon the Shakespeares was that the real value of the security appropriated by Lambert exceeded by at least one third the amount of the loan,[1] and that the "oppressor's wrong" was felt from within their own immediate family connection.

We can imagine the surprise and indignation of the Shakespeare household, and the energetic utterances of the future author of the *Merchant of Venice*. Prone as John Shakespeare was to litigation, it is a little remarkable that nothing of that sort was attempted during the life of Edmund Lambert, and the doubtful conjecture is that the latter must have given some satisfactory verbal assurance.[2]

[1] As afterwards agreed by both parties in the compromise under which twenty pounds more were to be paid in addition to the forty loaned.

[2] Outlines, ii. 203. Of this supposed "verbal assurance" there is not a particle of proof, direct or indirect. The failure of John Shakespeare, the chronic litigant, to litigate with Edmund Lambert, for the whole seven years of his lifetime, the disputed question of the mortgage forfeiture, remains without explanation, upon any other theory than that the Gibbs lease was part of a family arrangement to protect John Shakespeare's life interest in Asbies from his creditors. That Edmund Lambert was aware of the real character of the transaction is apparent from the significant dovetailing of the mortgage with the lease, the lease being made to commence on the precise day that the mortgage debt was to fall due. This covinous privity between the brothers-in-law gave Edmund Lambert what we should now call a "pull." It practically put John Shakespeare *hors de combat* during the other's life. No sooner was Edmund Lambert dead, and the secret buried with him, than John Shakespeare began at

Upon his death, as stated, in 1587, his son and heir, John Lambert, was threatened with legal proceedings, and according to John Shakespeare's account, had doubts as to the validity of his title. A negotiation followed with a view to a settlement. William Shakespeare was then twenty-three, had been married five years, had left his family and gone to London. There is documentary evidence that he was an immediate party to this negotiation, and although no fact in his biography is more satisfactorily established, none has been so slighted by his biographers.[1]

An agreement was reached on the 26th September, 1587, to the effect that John Lambert should retain the property upon paying John Shakespeare an additional twenty pounds, that John Shakespeare should not bring suit, and that he and his wife should give John Lambert what we should call a quitclaim deed, *in which their son William Shakespeare should unite.*

Why should the concurrence of William Shakespeare have been made a condition precedent to this arrangement? It was conjectured by Halli-

once to move upon his son and heir. That John Lambert, the son, was ignorant of the fraud, is inferrible from his reference to the lease as a *bona fide* transaction in his answer to the Shakespeares' bill in chancery. It may be thought singular that Edmund Lambert's knowledge should not, at some time during his life, have been communicated to his son, but every lawyer of much experience knows how apt people are to be reticent about such matters, even in their own families.

[1] Outlines, i. 91.

well-Phillipps, in the earlier editions of his work, that there was probably a marriage settlement of Mrs. Shakespeare's property, under which a vested remainder in Asbies might have been claimed by her children. This theory has been abandoned, but nothing substituted in its place.[1] Inquiry upon some other line is therefore in order, and perhaps all difficulty may be removed by considering the nature of the contemplated transaction, the circumstances of the principal parties, and their legal and equitable rights and relations.

It will be observed that the contention on the part of the Shakespeares was that the mortgage was never legally forfeited because the debt had been tendered when due. That being true, there was nothing to prevent their recovering the land by an action of ejectment. In that situation of affairs, any dealing between the mortgage creditor and debtor for a purchase of the debtor's interest was a ticklish business. The debtor was in necessitous circumstances. The transaction would be impeachable in equity upon the ground of constructive fraud, where Lambert would have been obliged to produce testimony to support its fairness, and especially the adequacy of the consideration. In the event of his parents' death, the same right to impeach the sale would devolve upon William Shakespeare, as oldest son and

[1] But see Appendix C for some considerations supporting the conjecture.

heir. Hence the supposed necessity for his being made a party.[1]

If that be the explanation, and no other has been advisedly suggested,[2] the future creator of Falstaff was fully aware of the fact that his participation in the compromise was suggested by a wholesome dread of equity on the part of Lambert's solicitor.

And now another disappointment awaited the unhappy Shakespeare family. So far they had only tasted the "oppressor's wrong." They were now to drain the cup to the bitter dregs. For some reason not explained, John Lambert reneged; repudiated his contract. It could hardly have been from pecuniary inability. There would have been no difficulty in raising the twenty pounds upon the security of the property. He may have concluded after all that there was practically little danger to his title, and that the Shakespeares would be unable to produce the requisite proof of the tender. He may have been advised that the purchase of the equity of redemption, under the circumstances, was still a risky transaction, even with the participation therein

[1] No reported case can be cited in which this principle, afterwards so familiar, had been distinctly acted upon at that time. *Conscience* was enough, without more, to suggest the doubt, and there was no telling, in those days, what the chancellor might do in the direction or upon the analogy of the well-known principle of the Roman law, "*tutor rem pupilli emere non potest.*" (1 Spence, Eq. 626.)

[2] But see Appendix C, for an alternative explanation.

of William Shakespeare. At all events, he concluded to keep his money and the land both, and John Shakespeare might sue and be happy. There was nothing else to be done. The only questions were: First, should the suit be to recover the land or the twenty pounds? and next, should the suit be in the Stratford court or in one of the superior courts of the metropolis?

The result of the family discussions was that an action of assumpsit was brought in the court of queen's bench in 1589 by John Shakespeare *v.* John Lambert, upon the latter's breach of contract in failing to pay the twenty pounds. From the declaration filed in this case, the foregoing particulars have been taken.[1]

[1] A copy in Latin is given in Outlines, ii. 11–13, reproduced in translation in Appendix B. In the induction to the *Taming of the Shrew* there are several allusions which indicate the probability of this case being in the author's mind at the time of its composition. According to Stokes, this comedy was produced before 1594, and according to Heraud, in 1592–1593. (Sto. Chron. Order, 54; Her. Life, 9.) Malone dates it 1594. When the page is presented to Sly as his wife, and Sly asks, "What must I call her? Al'ce madam, or Joan madam?" it is a little remarkable that in these two names are to be found the names of Edmund Lambert's wife and her maiden sister. Barton-on-the-Heath, the residence of Edmund Lambert, was otherwise spelled Burton. "Am not I Christopher Sly, old Sly's son of Burton-Heath?" may possibly have been a jibe at the expense of John Lambert, Edmund Lambert's son. The first suit of John Shakespeare *v.* John Lambert was brought in 1589 in the queen's bench to recover the sum of *twenty pounds* under an alleged compromise of the mortgage difficulty, to which the poet was himself a party. In the induction we have, "I would not

John Lambert, the defendant, by his attorney, pleads *non assumpsit*. Upon that plea issue is joined, and there the record ends. So far as appears, the case was never tried. That it was not settled is manifest from the sequel.

It may be assumed that there were the usual imparlances, essoigns, and continuances, such as made the "law's delay" one of the troubles which might drive reflecting men to contemplate suicide. But in all probability the case languished for want of funds. There is evidence that John Shakespeare had nothing; there is no evidence that his son in London had at that time anything to spare. Time stayed still with the "lawyers in the vacation, for they sleep between term and term."[1] The fees which could alone awaken them were hard to raise, and the "breath of an unfeed lawyer" was found to have "nothing" in it.[2] "Here 's a fish hangs in the net like a poor man's right in the law, 't will hardly come out."[3]

Shakespeare's attorney was a certain John Harborn. His conduct of the suit appears to have been satisfactory to the other side, since a

lose the dog for *twenty pound*." "And *twenty* caged nightingales do sing." "And *twenty* more such names and men as these." The same word is frequently repeated throughout the play. This last circumstance might seem trifling but for its connection with the others.

[1] *As You Like It*, Act III. scene 2. [2] *Lear*, Act I. scene 4.

[3] *Pericles*, Act II. scene 1.

few years later we find him acting as John Lambert's attorney in the same court in an ejectment suit with another party.[1]

The period of delay to which reference is now being made covers the later years of the first and obscure period of the dramatist's London life, from 1589, when the suit was begun, until his first audacious bid for popularity. Although the three parts of *Henry the Sixth* are supposed to have been produced with applause in 1592, the literary world was not fairly taken by storm until the appearance in 1593 of what he himself calls the "first heir of his invention," the daringly flesh-colored and sparingly fig-leaved *Venus and Adonis*.[2]

Of fame and fortune the vista now clearly opens before the youthful poet, and Lambert's twenty pounds look smaller than they did. At

[1] Adams *v.* Lambert, 4 Rep. 96. While looking into the reports in the course of this investigation, another curiosity turned up. One of the famous controversies of the day, the decision of which settled the action of assumpsit upon a firm basis, was Slade's case, reported by Coke, 4 Rep. 91. The courts being divided in opinion, the case was twice argued before all the judges of England. Francis Bacon was of counsel, and associated with him as attorney on the same side was a lawyer named *John Halstaff*. The case was pending from 1596 to 1602. When the author of the First Part of *Henry Fourth* found himself obliged in 1597 to find some other name to substitute for the offensive "Sir John Oldcastle," and to find it in a hurry, *did he get the suggestion of Sir John Falstaff from the name of John Halstaff?*

[2] Outlines, i. 97, 102.

the same time the Asbies estate is found to be increasing in value, and the Gibbs lease is within a few years of expiring. The project of obtaining for John Shakespeare a patent of gentility begins to be conceived. William Shakespeare's maternal inheritance, unjustly withheld by Lambert, would gracefully come in to support the character of "gentleman's son." In short, there were obvious reasons why the recovery of the land was to be preferred to the money.[1]

The action of assumpsit in the queen's bench[2] was accordingly abandoned (it does not appear

[1] In addition, there is a probability that the advice of counsel discouraged the prosecution of the action of assumpsit as not being well founded in point of law. This suggestion is based upon a decision of the very court in which the case of Shakespeare *v.* Lambert was pending, a year or two after that suit was instituted. That decision of the court of queen's bench was to the effect that the promise of an heir, in consideration of forbearance of a suit to which he was not liable, will not support an assumpsit. (Tooley *v.* Windham, Cro. Eliz. 206.) There was no allegation in the Shakespeares' *narr.* from which the court could determine the validity either of Lambert's "doubt" or of Shakespeare's threat to sue him. As soon as it was found that the action at law would of necessity involve the merits of the original controversy, viz., *the fact of the tender*, it was naturally deemed preferable to raise that question in a suit to recover the land itself.

[2] The learned reader will note, with some surprise, that a scholar so accurate and well-informed as Mr. Halliwell-Phillipps should have mistaken an action of assumpsit in the queen's bench for a bill in equity to enforce a specific performance, and especially that so palpable an *erratum* should have been allowed to pass uncorrected, through all the editions of his invaluable work. (Outlines, ii. 11.)

to have been formally dismissed), and the theatre of litigation was transferred to the other side of Westminster Hall, where the subject-matter of controversy was made the recovery of the land itself.

CHAPTER XVII

IN CHANCERY

Reasons for resorting to equity. — Two successive suits. — Coincidence of dates. — Bad pleading. — Failure of suit.

THE reason for preferring the court of chancery was not, as might be supposed, to avoid the legal effect of the alleged forfeiture. At that period the chancellor's jurisdiction had not advanced so far as to afford relief in such cases, unless some special circumstances of accident could be shown to excuse the default.[1] In this case there was no default to be excused, since none was admitted, the contention of the Shakespeares being that the forty pounds had been actually tendered when due. That claim, if substantiated, would support an action of ejectment. But an action at law was to be deprecated because it would of necessity involve a trial of the disputed issue of fact at *nisi prius* before a Warwickshire jury. Such a jury it was not the policy of the Shakespeares to face, by reason of local prejudice. John Shakespeare's career had

[1] 1 Spence, Eq. 603, 629, notes.

been too litigious not to have made many enemies whom his poverty had now let loose. His son's poaching adventures, with their unlucky incidents, had thrown into the wrong scale the powerful interest of the Lucy family. And so far as the predominating local influence of the Lamberts was concerned, we have it very distinctly asserted in the Shakespeares' bill of complaint,[1] that "the sayde John Lamberte ys of greate wealthe and abilitie, and well frended and alied amongest gentlemen and free holders of the countrey in the said countie of Warwicke, where he dwelleth, and your said oratours are of small wealthe and verey few frendes and alyance in the saide countie."[2]

Obviously, therefore, it was the policy of the Shakespeares to secure if possible the trial of the issue of fact upon testimony privately taken under commission, and to obtain its decision by the chancellor. In order, however, to enable the chancellor to assume jurisdiction, special circumstances were necessary to be alleged showing the impracticability of the legal remedy in the particular case. The facts of this nature relied on by the Shakespeares were (in addition to the adverse local influence of "the proud man's contumely") that the deeds and evidences of title were in the

[1] Appendix B.

[2] Outlines, ii. 14, 15. "In disgrace with fortune and men's eyes." (Sonnet 29.)

hands of the other side,[1] that Lambert had lately made secret conveyances to parties unknown, and that it was therefore impossible to tell against whom to bring actions at law.

We may well suppose that the course adopted was not finally decided upon without some correspondence between Stratford and London, and much conference between William Shakespeare and his London solicitor and possibly counsel. It may as well be stated at this point as at any other that as a matter of well-founded inference from known facts all the authorities are agreed that this whole Lambert litigation from beginning to end was backed by William Shakespeare to the extent of his means.[2]

It has already been stated that there were two chancery suits against John Lambert. One was in the name of John Shakespeare alone, the other was in the name of himself and wife. The second alone is extant. The bill appears to have been filed 24th November, 1597, and is given in full by Halliwell-Phillips, together with the answer and replication.[3]

[1] The detention of title deeds, preventing the plaintiff from making *profert*, and thus depriving him of his remedy at law, was a recognized ground of equitable jurisdiction. (Reeves, E. C. L. ii. 467.)

[2] Outlines, i. 149; Lee's Life of Shakespeare, 195.

[3] Outlines, ii. 14, etc. Reproduced in Appendix B. There is some question as to which of the two suits was first instituted. Halliwell-Phillipps supposes that the joint bill was the earliest, and this supposition is apparently sustained by the preamble to

Candor compels the reluctant admission that, from the Shakespeare standpoint, these chancery

the order of 18th of May, 1599. (Outlines, i. 150, ii. 204; Appendix B.) But this preamble evidently gets the cart before the horse. The bill first filed was the individual bill of John Shakespeare alone, as plainly appears from Lambert's answer to the joint bill of 24th November, 1597, wherein he begins by reserving all exceptions "for that the like byll, in effect contayning the self-same matter, hath byne *heretofore* exhibited into this honorable courte against this defendante, whereunto this deft. hath made a full and directe answeare, wherein the *said complainante* (singular, not plural) hath not proceeded to hearinge." That the preamble referred to is mistaken is apparent by simple comparison with the two preceding orders of 5th July and 10th July, 1598 (Outlines, ii. 204; Appendix B), both of which, as appears upon their face, were orders passed in the joint suit, although the preamble in question attributes them to the individual suit. It is probable that upon the Master's report that both bills were *ad idem*, the individual bill was dismissed prior to 27th June, 1599. Otherwise it is impossible to explain the order of that date following the "liberty to change commissions" reserved in the order of 18th May, 1599. It does not appear when the first bill was filed, except that it was long enough before November, 1597, to allow of an answer. For aught that appears, the first suit may have been pending for several years. It is referred to in Lambert's answer to the second or joint bill, and also in the order of 18th May, 1599, from both of which it may be gathered that both bills prayed in substance the same relief, viz., "to be relieved touching a mortgage of certain lands in the county of Warwick, made to the defendant's father, whose heir the defendant is." (Order of 18th May, 1599; Outlines, ii. 204, III.; Appendix B.) The first bill was certainly defective for want of a necessary party as co-plaintiff, viz., Mary Shakespeare, the owner of the inheritance, and it may have been defective in other respects. Why leave was not obtained to file an amended bill, or why the defective bill was not dismissed when the other was filed, are questions more easily asked than answered. The procedure was certainly anomalous, even for those days of crude equity pleading.

proceedings are, upon the whole, decidedly disappointing. As a piece of professional work, the bill of complaint is rather a slovenly performance, not very creditable to solicitor Powle, or to whomsoever else may have been the draftsman. It contrasts unfavorably with Lambert's answer, both in point of substance and form. In the stating part of the bill, where we look for most precision and certainty of averment, we are surprised to find no dates given, no reference whatever to documents (the indenture, feoffment, and fine), and, as to the mortgage transaction, a reference not only vague but inaccurate, so erroneous indeed that it is open to flat contradiction by the records specifically set forth in the answer. We are still more surprised to notice that the vital fact of the *tender*, the pivot upon which the whole controversy turned, is stated in such terms as in effect to put the plaintiffs out of court at once. Instead of the tender being claimed as made on the day limited in the indenture, which was within less than two years from its date, it is vaguely stated to be after the space of "three or fower yeares." The answer having presented a distinct issue, by the precise denial of a tender made upon the day limited in the indenture, the plaintiffs, in their replication, for the first time claim a tender made upon that day, in palpable inconsistency with the previous averment of the bill. The same reckless incoherency is observable in the statement of the person or persons making the tender; it being alleged in one place that it was made by both plaintiffs jointly, and afterwards by John Shakespeare alone. The apology offered by Mr. Halliwell-Phillipps for these conspicuous "deviations from the precise facts" must be admitted to be feeble and unsatisfactory. He says they "may be reasonably explained as due to *imperfect recollections*." [1] The fact is that these blunders could easily have been avoided by reference to the declaration in the queen's bench, where the transaction was correctly set forth.

The end of the case is such as might be expected from so inauspicious a beginning. From orders passed in the last year but one of the century it appears that a commission was issued to examine witnesses on both sides, that testimony was accordingly taken, and publication thereof passed.[2]

Who the witnesses were, or what the evidence was, does not appear, except that it was of such a character that the cause was never brought to a hearing, but was permitted to slumber indefinitely, while the Lamberts meanwhile retained possession of Asbies.

[1] Outlines, ii. 370, No. 323.

[2] Ib. 204, 205; Appendix B.

CHAPTER XVIII

NEW PLACE

Another coincidence in dates. — Reconstructing New Place while constructing Falstaff. — Fourth and last interpretation. — Probable allusion to the pending suit. — Conclusion.

In order to get a connected view of this litigation we have been obliged to anticipate. In the year 1597, the controversy was not only alive, but the new bill filed in November of that year shows that it was "stirring."

For all the purposes of this present inquiry, it is immaterial whether these chancery proceedings were instituted by the Shakespeares in good faith, with an expectation of being able to substantiate their position (that a tender of the mortgage debt had actually been made at the time and place required), or whether the whole effort was, as charged by Lambert in his answer, a mere game of bluff, "thinking thereby, as it should seem, to wring from this deft. some further recompense from the said premises than they had already received."[1] In the view of equity

[1] Outlines, ii. 16; Appendix B.

jurisprudence as it exists to-day, and as it has been administered since the time of Charles I., the Shakespeares had not lost their right of redemption, even if they failed to prove tender or payment on the day.[1] Although in their time equity was visibly "stirring," it had not yet stirred deeply enough into the odious law of forfeitures to secure that common justice to Shakespeare's parents which subsequently became familiar relief in like cases.

There are circumstances which lend some degree of probability to the Shakespeare side of the controversy. Before the mortgage debt matured, the fund to meet it appears to have been provided. Forty pounds were realized by the sale of Mrs. Shakespeare's reversionary interest in some copyhold land left by her father at Snitterfield,[2] and four pounds from the sale of John Shakespeare's individual share in certain property at the same place.[3]

The point of this discussion, however, is not as to the merits of the controversy, or whether the contention of the Shakespeares was well or ill founded, but as to the meaning of Falstaff's "equity stirring," and whether or not that ex-

[1] 1 Spence, Eq. 603.

[2] Outlines, i. 59. The fine levied on the occasion is dated in Easter term, 1580. (Outlines, ii. 176, par. III.)

[3] Outlines, ii. 179. This sale was in October, 1579. The Lambert mortgage debt fell due, as has been stated, 29 September, 1580.

pression is to be interpreted, at least in part, in the light of the circumstances referred to.

The coincidence of dates is clearly established. The chancery suit referred to was beyond all question pending at the time the First Part of *Henry IV.* was under construction. Three months before the piece was entered for publication we find an important movement made in the progress of the litigation, the filing of an entirely new bill of complaint, introducing a new party, that party the mother of William Shakespeare. The step was doubtless taken advisedly, after correspondence with Stratford and consultation with counsel. The suit involved the maternal inheritance of William Shakespeare. At an earlier stage of the business he had personally mixed up in it, as a party to a proposed compromise. He was now the promoter of the litigation, his own purse its only banker. It was a family quarrel of long standing, and a bitter one.

Further, it has already been shown that nine days before the filing of the new bill in Shakespeare *v.* Lambert, an important decision of the twelve judges of England was announced by the chancellor in another case pending at the same time, in principle analogous.[1] One involved the forfeiture of a mortgage; the other the forfeiture of a lease; and both for an alleged default in payment at the day. In both, equitable relief

[1] Throckmorton *v.* Finch, *supra.*

was sought. In Throckmorton *v.* Finch, that relief was denied, solely because there had been a judgment at law. In Shakespeare *v.* Lambert, no such obstacle had intervened. From this it may be inferred that the revival of the latter suit, so soon after the decision in the other, was not only *post hoc*, but *propter hoc*. In other words, Shakespeare felt encouraged by that decision to go on with his parents' suit. Not only that, — it would gratify them, especially his mother, to find the great subject of domestic anxiety reflected in words of cheer and assurance from the very theatre of their son's success. "There 's no equity stirring," as used in Falstaff's adjuration, means of course there *is* equity stirring. The action at law had miscarried, the first chancery suit had languished, the old folks were beginning to get discouraged. He would "pick flint, and try it again." It was now to be dropped, and a new suit commenced. Lambert need not flatter himself that equity was dead or asleep. He would find it "stirring." Lambert need not suppose from our failure to push the old suit, that we have despaired of our equity of redemption in Asbies. He will soon hear from this new suit, that we are about to bring to the chancellor's attention, that the old equity of redemption, "this downtrodden equity,"[1] is still alive and "stirring."

[1] *King John*, Act. II. scene 1.

It is true that this personal allusion would not be taken by the general public, and would not contribute to stage effect. There has already been found in the expression quite enough for those purposes. In the sense of the term now under consideration, the author had in view a small and more select circle, and one of much more interest to himself,— his own family, the Lambert connection, the lawyers on both sides, and the entire Stratford community, among whom this chronic litigation between the Shakespeares and the Lamberts had long been village gossip. In addition, it is likely that there was also a shrewd bid for the notice of the lord chancellor himself.

It may be objected that it is impossible to tell with certainty what may have been in the author's mind, and that all this is mere speculation, incapable of positive proof. It is true that this is one of those questions incapable of mathematical demonstration, but there is nothing speculative in the data from which the inference is drawn. Those data are all matters of record. It is upon the strength of those authentic premises that certain questions naturally arise. Is the expression fairly susceptible of the meaning attributed to it? Is it used elsewhere by the writer with a similar signification? Is there in the past life of the writer such an experience as would make the particular use in the present connection antecedently probable? Are the circumstances surrounding the writer at the time such as would make such use natural and appropriate? Has the writer a special proclivity for the use of terms in different senses at once? Is he a writer from whom might naturally be expected, upon occasion, a subtle undercurrent of sly personal allusion? These inquiries suggest the elements from which the conclusion indicated may with at least reasonable probability be drawn. That is all there is contended for. To require nothing short of absolute certainty in such cases would put an end to all historical, all biographical, and all antiquarian research.

Here we are not left to vague inference or conjecture from mere generalities. Another significant coincidence in dates remains to be noticed, bringing to bear an authentic piece of personal testimony, of pointed and persuasive, if not absolutely conclusive, force. "The chief fact of interest in the personal annals of this year, 1597, is the remarkable circumstance that Shakespeare, after leaving his native town in indigence only seven years previously, should now have been enabled to become, so far as material advantages were concerned, one of its leading inhabitants."[1]

The reference, of course, is to the purchase of "New Place," the "great house," as it was called

[1] Outlines, i. 133.

by Sir Hugh Clopton, for whom it was built a century before, the "great house," as it was thenceforth popularly known in Stratford.[1] Being in a dilapidated condition, Shakespeare acquired it at a bargain, and immediately began the work of restoration. He repaired the house, replanted the orchard, and improved the grounds. It was in the garden that he afterwards planted the famous "mulberry tree."

The purchase was completed in the spring of the same memorable year, 1597, while equity was stirring and shaking Westminster Hall with Homeric, or rather Elizabethan laughter, in the person of the unlucky scrivener, with his bare head protruding through the hole cut by the chancellor's order in his too voluminous replication in the chancery case of Mylward *v.* Weldon; while equity was stirring the whole public through the sensational episode of the reference by the queen to the twelve judges of England of the chancery case of Throckmorton *v.* Finch; while equity was stirring Shakespeare himself in the new face about to be put upon the old chancery

[1] It had a frontage of over sixty feet, with proportionate depth, and numerous apartments, no fewer than ten of them provided with fireplaces. The so-called "great garden" inclosed an area of three quarters of an acre, with barns, stables, and outhouses. There is evidence that Shakespeare began to occupy the residence shortly after its purchase from William Underhill. The transaction was consummated by the usual levy of a fine, a curious facsimile of which is to be seen in Outlines, ii. 106. See, also, ib. 105, 110, 124.

suit of Shakespeare *v.* Lambert. During this period the successful playwright is found making his first investment in Stratford real estate; negotiating for the purchase of the finest property in the borough; making trips to Stratford to look at it; busy with conveyancers, solicitors, surveyors, architects, builders, contractors, gardeners, and laborers; paying their bills, big and little; superintending their work from time to time; his mind delighting in the task of making a home for his separated family, and a haven of tranquil retirement for himself.[1]

With his most congenial thoughts thus fixed on his native nest and the acquisition of a permanent residence in Stratford, he is still at work in his profession, casting the immortal Falstaff; mentally blocking out scenes, conceiving situations, devising plots, constructing incidents, manipulating characters, premeditating dialogue; his mind all on fire with sally and repartee, on fire with the impact of a storm of suggestions, the great majority of them rejected, the select few retained, mused over, elaborated, always with the vision before him of the audience whose approbation was to him fame and fortune.

1 "Lord! who would live turmoiled in the court,
And may enjoy such quiet walks as these?
I seek not to wax great by others' waning,
Or gather wealth, I care not with what envy:
Sufficeth that I have maintains my state,
And sends the poor well pleased from my gate."
(*2 Henry VI.* Act IV. scene 10.)

A more select audience, and to him personally a far more interesting one, is also present not only to his mind, but to his bodily eyes, at the same instant. The home people among whom his childhood was passed; who are again to be his neighbors; whom he chats with as they pass by the gate of his New Place yard, where they find him with his hands full; who, for want of a topic, bother him with their simple questions about that old Lambert business, and how the chancery suit is coming on, and when he expects to get it tried, and what are the prospects for the old folks getting back their Asbies farm; these Stratford burgesses and aldermen and common people are also to have at least a passing recognition. He will have Falstaff let them know that the Asbies business is all right. Equity is stirring in that quarter also, as Lambert will soon find when the new bill is ready.

The inference from this circumstance, in connection with the others already named, may safely be left to the intelligence of the reader. It is seldom that a proposition, speculative in its nature, such as the question of an author's state of mind in relation to a particular subject-matter, and his mental intent in the use of a particular expression, can be found sustained by circumstantial evidence so nearly approaching demonstration as the proof in support of the proposition that in Falstaff's "equity stirring" the writer had in view, incidentally, of course, and by the wind of the shot, as it were, his Stratford neighbors as the audience, the Lambert suit as the subject, and the Asbies inheritance as the object.

Shortly before the purchase of New Place, we have the first evidence of the poet's rising pecuniary fortunes and of his determination to advance in social position, in the grant of coat-armor to John Shakespeare, obtained at his son's expense in October, 1596.[1] The natural connection between this attempt "to confer gentility on the family" and the effort to secure by litigation the restoration of the coveted maternal inheritance, has been already noticed. All these circumstances are significant as revealing the playwright's state of mind and presumed intent in using the language referred to. Any construction put upon the expression "no equity stirring" which would wholly exclude these circumstances from just consideration, and ignore the mental attitude they indicate, would be liable to suspicion at best, if not rejected as inadequate and misleading. On the other hand, the construction here offered dovetails exactly with all existing facts, and takes its color from the immediate surroundings.

> "Our poesy is as a gum, which oozes
> From whence 't is nourished. The fire i' the flint
> Shows not, till it be struck."[2]

[1] Outlines, i. 130.

[2] *Timon of Athens*, Act I. scene 1.

We have now walked all around Falstaff's neglected appeal to "equity stirring," and have found it four-square, like a house. Its front, as seen from the great highway of the ages, needs no special interpretation. All who pass by hastily will read it, as all who have gone by hastily have read it, to refer simply to the one idea of abstract justice. That is enough for the million. Let them pass. Let them still follow the silent procession of commentators, without a look or a word of intelligent appreciation. But to those who have the time and the taste to linger and explore, there are two gable-end aspects, one of rare historical interest, the other a unique and comical curiosity; and besides these, somewhat more obscurely seen in the rear, a domestic view over Shakespeare's back-yard, rather too quaint, it must be admitted, for modern admiration.

There may be minds so constituted as to find it difficult to admit that this, or any other expression, could have been used, even by Shakespeare, in four distinct senses at once. With any such, there need be no quarrel. Each of the interpretations suggested is entirely independent of the others. If they are supposed to crowd each other, let the fittest survive. But before rejecting either, let it at least be fully realized that we are dealing with an exceptional author whose intellectual habit it was to exhaust the meaning of the words he handled, and for that purpose to select words rich in meaning. Here he does not have to go out of his way to lug in by the ears some "forged quaint conceit," questionable quibble, or preposterous pun. He finds a covey right before him, and he brings down four birds at a shot.

The complex jest is exploded, and then the delighted fancy of the author flies off on another excursion in a different direction. "There 's no more valor in that Poins than in a wild duck." Swiftly upon that, rush in the Prince and Poins, those same "arrant cowards," sword in hand. "Your money!" "Villains!" One or two passes are exchanged, and off waddles the sweating Falstaff, with his "equity" and his "wild duck," "larding the lean earth as he walks along," with reluctant backward glances, leaving his plunder behind, and with it, "argument for a week, laughter for a month, and a good jest forever."[1]

[1] *1 Henry IV.* Act II. scene 2.

APPENDIX A

THE WAR BETWEEN THE COURTS.—CHRONOLOGY

THE genesis of the controversy is traced to the great struggle between the laws of England and Rome, from the twelfth century to the fourteenth, when it merges into the long contest with the constantly developing jurisdiction of chancery, settled finally by the intervention of King James the First on the side of chancery in 1616. (*Ante*, p. 28.)

Temp. King Stephen, A. D. 1135–1154. Study of Roman civil law introduced at Oxford by Vacarius. Prohibited by royal proclamation.[1]

Henry II., 1154–1189. Violent struggle for jurisdiction between the laws of England and Rome, resulting in clipping the wings of the ecclesiastical courts by the Constitutions of Clarendon, followed by the assassination of archbishop and ex-chancellor Thomas à Becket. Constitutions of Clarendon annulled by Pope Alexander III.[2]

John, 1199–1216. The barons declare for trial by jury and the law of the land.[3]

Magna Charta annulled by Pope Innocent III. and its supporters excommunicated.[4]

Henry III., 1216–1272. The barons reply to the prelates, "Quod nolunt leges Angliæ mutare." They are un-

[1] 1 Bl. Com. 19; 1 Pollock & Maitland, History of English Law, 98.

[2] 4 Bl. Com. 422; 1 Pol. & M. 104; 1 Stubbs, Constitutional History of England, ch. xii.; Hallam, M. A. ch. vii.; Camp. Life of Becket.

[3] Magna Charta.

[4] 2 Stubbs, ch. xiv.; 1 Hume, 434, 5; 3 Lingard, 52.

willing to change the common for the civil law.[1] Magna Charta confirmed. Bracton.

Edward I., 1272–1307. Stubborn opposition to continued encroachment of ecclesiastical courts. Vigorous measures taken to repress it.[2]

Edward III., 1327–1377. Struggle over jurisdiction renewed. Wyclif and the Lollards. Chaucer. By a royal ordinance, 22 Edw. III., all matters "of grace" referred to the chancellor. Statute of *premunire*, 27 Edw. III. (so called from the leading word in the writ by which sheriff is charged to summon delinquents), denouncing with severe penalties those "which do sue in any other court to defeat or impeach the judgments given in the king's court." This is the statute mainly relied on by the common law judges in their opposition to the equity jurisdiction of restraining judgments by injunction.[3] The Roman law, heretofore in favor with the courts, now becomes an object of aversion.[4] Lords and commons complain that the state had been too long governed by churchmen, and petition that none but laymen be appointed chancellor.[5]

Richard II., 1377–1399. Increase of Lollardry. The barons protest that they will never suffer the kingdom to be governed by the Roman law. The judges prohibit the citation of the civil law. Effect of the exclusion of the civil law from the common law courts, to throw the exclusive administration of *trusts* into the court of chancery. Waltham supposed to devise the writ of subpœna, 1386. Jealousy of Parliament toward the growing power of chancery. Repeated efforts to restrain and limit its authority. Its jurisdiction supported by the crown. Parliament will not admit of an equity of redemption.[6]

[1] Stat. of Merton.

[2] 4 Bl. Com. 425.

[3] 3 Inst. 119, 122.

[4] 1 Spence, Eq. 346.

[5] Camp. Lives Chan., "Wickham."

[6] 2 Fon. Eq. iii. 1, sec. 2, note; 1 Spence, Eq. 346; 3 Bl. Com. 52; 4 Inst. 82; 3 Reeves, Hist. C. L. 188, 274, 379; Parkes, Hist. Chan. 39–48; Gilb. For. Rom. 17; 1 Sto. Eq. Jur. sec. 46; 1 Pom. Eq. sec. 20; Camp. Lives Ch. of R. II.

Henry IV., 1399–1413. Lollards persecuted and Sir John Oldcastle executed. Continued struggle against the growing jurisdiction of equity. The commons renew their petitions complaining of the court of chancery, particularly of its interference with matters remediable at law. Statute of Prohibition, 4 Henry IV., declaring that judgments at law should not be annulled excepting by attaint or for error, one of the statutes afterwards relied on by the judges to support their opposition to common injunctions.[1]

Henry V., 1413–1422. The same struggle continues. The commons renew their remonstrances against the court of chancery, which is again supported by the crown.[2]

Henry VI., 1422–1461. The struggle continues. In this feeble reign, the chancellors fail of their accustomed support from the crown. The opposition to chancery scores a point in securing the passage of an act requiring that no subpœna should issue in matters determinable by the common law, and requiring a certificate by two justices, and bond to be given by all plaintiffs in equity.[3]

This statute appears to have been neglected by the chancellors, since it was again distinctly provided that "no matter determinable by the law of this realm" shall be "determined in other form than after the course of the same law in the king's courts."[4]

Edward IV., 1461–1483. In this despotic reign the court of chancery is firmly in the saddle. No further opposition is made in Parliament, and the struggle is transferred to the courts of law. The right of the chancellor to restrain judgments by injunction "vehemently opposed," as appears by the Year Books. In 5 Edw. IV. 35, it was resolved that after judgment at common law the party could not be relieved in equity. In 22 Edw. IV. 37, the same was again

[1] 4 Inst. 83; Doctor and Student, ch. xviii.; 3 Bl. Com. 52; 1 Spence, Eq. 348; and authorities cited *supra*.

[2] Camp. Life of Beaufort, and same authorities.

[3] 15 H. VI.

[4] 31 H. VI. c. 2; 4 Inst. 83, 84; 1 Spence, Eq. 370.

resolved, with the declaration by the judges that they would release on *habeas corpus* any suitor who should be imprisoned by the chancellor for breach of such an injunction.[1]

Henry VIII., 1509-1547. Lollardry merging into Puritanism. Impeachment of Cardinal Wolsey for (amongst other articles) assuming jurisdiction as chancellor after judgment at law. Continued opposition of the judges to injunctions granted by his successor, Sir Thomas More. He proposes to the judges that if they would "mitigate and reform the rigor of the law themselves, there would be no more injunctions." They refuse, and he announces his purpose to persevere. Stat. of Uses, 27 H. VIII., designed to abolish equitable jurisdiction over landed property, but such effect defeated by narrow decisions.[2]

Elizabeth, 1558–1603. "The warfare between the two sides of Westminster Hall" (in the language of Lord Campbell) continues throughout this reign, as shown by the following cases, cited 3 Inst. 124: Mich., 8 & 9 El., in B. R. Ralph Heydon, gent., was indicted of a *premunire* upon the stat. 27 Edw. III., for procuring of Sir Nicholas Bacon, Lord Keeper of the Great Seal, to grant an injunction in chancery after judgment given in ejectment, in subversion of the laws of the realm; Trin., 21 El., in the common pleas a writ of *premunire* upon the said stat. of 27 Edw. III. by Beans against Lloyd, for suing before the president and council in Wales (a court of equity) after judgment in the common pleas, in subversion, etc.; Pasch., 27 El., in B. R. Peter Dewse was indicted for procuring an injunction in chancery after a judgment in ejectment; Trin., 30 El., in B. R. John Heal, of the Inner Temple, Esquire, was indicted of a *premunire* for procuring a suit in chancery after a judgment at law, contrary to stat. 27 Edw. III. On exceptions

[1] 3 Inst. 123; Cro. Jac. 344.

[2] 2 Bl. Com. 336; 4 Reeves' Hist. C. L. 520, 370–376; Parkes' Hist. Chan. 63, 65; Roper, Life of More, 42; Camp. do.; 1 Sto. Eq. Jur. sec. 51; 3 Inst. 124; 4 Inst. 91.

taken by counsel, the court resolved that the court of chancery was within the statute of *premunire*, but quashed the indictment for a variance in the name of a party. The court's retreat was the result of a stir which brought down upon the judges the wrath of Queen Elizabeth.[1]

A few years later, an ejectment case, in which Queen Elizabeth was personally interested in maintaining an iniquitous judgment in favor of her grantee, was brought into chancery upon a bill to restrain the judgment by injunction. The case being referred, over the chancellor's head, to the twelve judges of England by the order of the queen,[2] they unanimously decided that the injunction should not issue, upon the broad ground that, after judgment at law there could be no relief in equity.[3]

James I., 1603–1625. Nothing daunted by this array of authority, because certain of the royal support, Ellesmere, after the accession of James I., took occasion to lay down the doctrine which has ever since prevailed, that "where a judgment is obtained by oppression, wrong, and a hard conscience, the chancellor will frustrate and set it aside, not for any error or defect in the judgment, but for the hard conscience of the party."[4]

Through the efforts of Bacon and Ellesmere, this doctrine was finally established by a prerogative order of James I.;[5] and shortly afterwards Lord Coke, the cham-

[1] *Ante*, chapter v.

[2] May 28, 1597.

[3] Throckmorton *v.* Finch, 3 Inst. 124; 4 Inst. 86; Cro. Jac. 344; Appendix to 1 Rep. Ch. 40–42; *ante*, p. 48.

[4] Earl of Oxford's case, 1 Ch. Rep. 1; 2 Lead. Ca. in Eq. 601.

[5] 18 July, 1616; 1 Cary's Rep. 163. The crisis was precipitated by the action of the judges, Coke especially, in the following cases: Heath *v.* Ridley, Cro. Jac. 335; Courtney *v.* Glanvil, Cro. Jac. 343; Goge's case, 1 Rolle, 277. A commission of crown lawyers, with Bacon at its head, was instructed to report as to the precedents. The commission reported that the chancery "does not assume to undo the judgment, but only to restrain the corrupt conscience of the party." Upon this report, the prerogative order was passed.

pion of the common law side of the controversy, was removed from the chief-justiceship of the court of king's bench.[1]

Later in the seventeenth century, the appellate jurisdiction of the house of lords over the court of chancery became firmly settled,[2] thus removing all occasion for further dispute.

The fact that the decrees of the chancellor were open to review and reversal by an assemblage of laymen, practically controlled by lawyers advanced by their ability to the peerage, had its effect in quieting apprehension of further undue encroachments of equity.[3]

[1] Camp. Lives C. J. ch. viii. Years afterwards, in his Institutes, Coke stubbornly repudiates the prerogative order as flatly illegal. 3 Inst. 125.

[2] 1 Spence, Eq. 396; 3 Bl. Com. 455.

[3] Much of the above is taken from the writer's "Juridical Equity."

APPENDIX B

DOCUMENTS PERTAINING TO THE SEVERAL CASES OF SHAKESPEARE *v.* LAMBERT

1. FINE levied, 1579, to assure the Lambert mortgage,[1] in the COURT OF COMMON PLEAS.

This is the final agreement, made in the Court of the lady the queen at Westminster, Easter term, in the twenty-first year of the reign of Elizabeth, by the grace of God, of England, France and Ireland queen, defender of the faith, and so forth, in the year of our Lord 1579, before James Dyer, Roger Manwood, Robert Munson and Thomas Meade, justices, and other faithful subjects of the lady the queen then there present, between Edmund Lambert complainant, and John Shakespere and Mary his wife, deforciants, of two messuages, two gardens, fifty acres of land, two acres of meadow, four acres of pasture, and common of pasture for cattle of all sorts, with the appurtenances, in Awston Cawntlett. Whereupon a plea of covenant was summoned between them &c., to wit, that the aforesaid John and Mary have acknowledged the aforesaid tenements and common of pasture with the appurtenances, to be the right of him the said Edmund, as those which the said Edmund hath of the gift of the aforesaid John and Mary, and those they have remised and quitted claim from them John and Mary and their heirs to the aforesaid Edmund, and his heirs forever. And further the same John and

[1] Translated from Latin in Outlines, ii. 11, the preamble being adapted from ii. 202. See 2 Bl. Com. Appendix, iv. 5. The other instruments of the transaction (indenture and deed-poll) are non-extant. *Ante*, pp. 117–119.

Mary have granted for themselves, and for the heirs of the said Mary, that they will warrant to the aforesaid Edmund and his heirs, the aforesaid tenements and common of pasture, with the appurtenances against the aforesaid John and Mary, forever. And for this recognition, remise, quitclaim, warranty, fine, etc., the said Edmund hath given to the said John and Mary forty pounds sterling.

2. In the Court of Queen's Bench. Michaelmas Term, 31–32 Eliz. (1589). John Shakespeare *v.* John Lambert.

Action, *assumpsit*, to recover damages for breach of contract of 26 September, 1587, for settlement of mortgage difficulty.

Declaration.[1]

Warwickshire: — Be it remembered that heretofore, to wit, at the term of Saint Michael last past, before the lady the queen at Westminster came John Shackespere by John Harborne, his attorney, and brought here into the court of the said lady the queen then and there his certain bill in a plea of trespass on the case against John Lambert, son and heir of Edmund Lambert late of Barton-on-the-Heath in the county aforesaid yeoman, in the custody of the marshall &c. and there are pledges of prosecution, to wit, John Doe and Richard Roe which said bill follows in these words: — Warr:, John Shackespere complains of John Lambert, son and heir of Edmund Lambert, late of Barton-on-the-Heath in the county aforesaid yeoman, in the custody of the marshall of the lady the queen's Marshalsea, before the queen herself that now is, for that, to wit, that whereas the said Edmund Lambert in his lifetime, to wit, on the fourteenth day of November in the twentieth year of the reign of

[1] Translated from Latin in Outlines, ii. 12. The importance of this document is that it brings in *William Shakespeare* as a contracting party, — the only authentic notice of the great dramatist between the years 1585 and 1592 which has yet been discovered.

Elizabeth now queen of England, by a certain indenture bearing date the day and year aforesaid, had bought unto himself and his heirs from the aforesaid John Shackespere and Mary, his wife, one messuage or tenement, one yard of land and four acres of arable land with the appurtenances in Wilmecote in the said county of Warwick, to have and to hold the aforesaid messuage or tenement and other the premises with the appurtenances, unto the said Edmund, his heirs, and assigns forever; provided always that if the said John Shackespere, his heirs, executors, administrators or assigns should pay or cause to be paid to the aforesaid Edmund forty pounds lawful English money on the feast day of Saint Michael the Archangel which then should be in the year of the Lord one thousand five hundred and eighty, that then and thereafter the aforesaid indenture and everything therein contained shall become void; by virtue of which the said Edmund entered into the aforesaid tenements with the appurtenances and was therein seised in his demesne as of fee, and being therein so seised, thereafter, to wit, on the first day of March of the twenty ninth year of the reign of the now lady the queen, died at the aforesaid Barton-on-the-Heath, after whose death the aforesaid messuage and other the premises with the appurtenances descended to the said John Lambert, as son and heir of the said Edmund; and the said John Lambert doubting his estate and interest of and in the said tenements with the appurtenances to be void and having notice that the aforesaid John Shackespere desired and intended to sue him for the premises, in consideration that the said John Shackespere then and thereafter should not sue the said John Lambert for the said messuage and other the premises with the appurtenances; and that the said John Shackespere and Mary, his wife, together with WILLIAM SHACKESPERE, his son, when thereto required, should assure to the said John Lambert the said messuage and other the premises with the appurtenances, and should deliver all writings and evidences concerning the aforesaid premises; the aforesaid John Lambert on the twenty sixth day of September in the twenty ninth year of the reign of the said lady the queen, at Stratford-on-Avon in the county aforesaid, in consideration thereof took upon himself and there and then promised faithfully to the said John Shackespere that he, the said John Lambert would well and truly pay and satisfy twenty pounds of lawful English money to the said John Shackespere in manner and form following, to wit, at and on the eighteenth day of November then next following twenty shillings, at and on the twenty third day of the same month three pounds, and at and on the fourth day of December then next following sixteen pounds, the residue of the aforesaid twenty pounds, at the dwelling house of one Anthony Ingram, gentleman, situate and being in Little Walford in the county aforesaid; and the aforesaid John Shackespere in fact says that he hitherto has not sued the said John Lambert for the premises nor any parcel thereof, and further that he the said John Shackespere and Mary, his wife, together with WILLIAM SHACKESPERE, his son, were always hitherto ready as well to assure the said premises as to deliver to the said John Lambert all writings and evidences concerning the said premises; nevertheless the said John Lambert, not regarding his said promise and undertaking, but contriving and fraudulently intending him the said John Shackespere of the said twenty pounds craftily and subtilely to deceive and defraud, contrary to his promise and undertaking hath not hitherto paid the said twenty pounds to the said John Shackespere, nor did he otherwise satisfy him for the same although thereunto often requested by the said John Shackespere thereafter, to wit, on the first day of September in the thirtieth year of the reign of the said lady the queen at Barton-on-the-Heath aforesaid in the county aforesaid, whereby the said John Shackespere hath wholly lost and missed the entire gain, advantage and profit which he by buying and bargaining with the aforesaid twenty pounds could have had and gained, to the damage of the said John Shackespere of thirty pounds, and thereupon he brings suit. — And now at this day, to wit, on the Tuesday next after the octave of Saint Michael in this same term until which day the aforesaid John Lambert had leave to imparle and then to answer &c. to the bill, before the lady the queen at Westminster come as well the aforesaid John Shackespere, by his attorney aforesaid, as the aforesaid John Lambert, by John Boldero, his attorney, and the said John Lambert defends the force and injury when, etc. and says that he has not taken upon himself in manner and form as the said John Shackespere has above against him declared, and thereof he puts himself upon the country; and the said John Shackespere likewise, etc. Therefore let a jury come before the lady the queen at Westminster on the Friday next after the octave of Saint Hillary, and who etc. to recognize etc., because as well etc. The same day is there given to the parties aforesaid etc.

3. In the High Court of Chancery. John Shakespeare, and his wife, Mary, *v.* John Lambert.

Bill in Chancery.[1]

24 Nov., 1597. To the righte honorable Sir Thomas Egerton, knighte, lorde keeper of the great seale of Englande. — In most humble wise complayninge, sheweth unto your good lordshippe your dailye oratours, John Shakespere of Stratford-upon-Avon, in the county of Warwicke, and Mary his Wief, that, whereas your saide oratours were lawfully seised in their demesne as of fee, as in the righte of the saide Mary, of and in one mesuage and one yarde lande with thappurtenaunces, lyinge and beinge in Wylnecote, in the saide county; and they beinge thereof so seised, for and in consideracion of the somme of fowerty poundes to them by one Edmounde Lamberte, of Barton-on-the-Heath in the

[1] Outlines, ii. 14; *post*, 170, note.

saide countie paide, your sayde oratours were contente that he, the saide Edmounde Lamberte, shoulde have and enjoye the same premisses until suche tyme as your saide oratours did repaie unto him the saide somme of fowertie poundes; by reason whereof the saide Edmounde did enter into the premisses and did occupie the same for the space of three or fower yeares, and thissues and profytes thereof did receiyve and take; after which your saide oratours did tender unto he saide Edmounde the sayde somme of fowerty poundes, and desired that hey mighte have agayne the sayde premisses accordinge to theire agreement; which money he the sayde Edmounde then refused to receyve, sayinge that he woulde not receyve the same, nor suffer your saide oratours to have the saide premisses agayne, unlesse they woulde paye unto him certayne other money which they did owe unto him for other matters; all which notwithstandinge, nowe so yt ys; and yt maye please yur good lordshippe that shortelie after the tendringe of the sayde fowertie poundes to the saide Edmounde, and the desyre of your sayde oratours to have theire lande agayne from him, he the saide Edmounde att Barton aforesayde dyed, after whose deathe one John Lamberte, as sonne and heire of the saide Edmounde, entred into the saide premisses and occupied the same; after which entrie of the sayde John your said oratours came to him and tendred the saide money unto him, and likewise requested him that he woulde suffer them to have and enjoye the sayde premisses accordinge to theire righte and tytle therein and the promise of his saide fathe to your saide oratours made, which he, the saide John, denyed in all thinges, and did withstande them for entringe into the premisses, and as yet doeth so contynewe still; and by reasone that certaine deedes and other evydences concerninge the premisses, and that of righte belonge to your saide oratours, are coumme to the handes and possession of the sayde John, he wrongfullie still keepeth and detayneth the possession of the saide premisses from your saide oratours, and will in noe wise permytt and suffer them to have and enjoye the sayde premisses accordinge to theire righte in and to the same; and he, the saide John Lamberte, hathe of late made sondrie secreate estates of the premisses to dyvrs persones to your said oratours unknowen, whereby your saide oratours cannot tell againste whome to bringe theire accions att the comen lawe for he recovery of the premisses; in tender consideracion whereof, and for so muche as your saide oratours knowe not the certaine dates nor contentes of thesaide wrytinges, nor whether he same be contayned in bagge, boxe or cheste, sealed, locked or noe, and therefore have no remeadie to recover the same evydences and wrytinges by the due course of the comen lawes of this realme; and forthat also, by reasone of the saide secreate estates so made by the saide John Lamberte as aforesaide, and want of your saide oratours havinge of the evidences and wrytinges as aforesaide, your sayde oratours cannot tell what accions or against whome or in what manner to bring their accion for the recoverie of the premisses att the comen lawe; and for that also the sayde John Lamberte ys of greate wealthe and abilitie, and well frended and alied amongest gentlemen and freeholders of the countrey in the saide countie of Warwicke, where he dwelleth, and your saide oratours are of small wealthe and verey few frendes and alyance in the said countie, maye yt therefore please your good lordshippe to graunt unto your saide oratours the Queenes Majesties moste gracyous writte of subpena, to be directed to the saide John Lamberte, commandinge him thereby at a certaine daie, and under a certain payne therein to be lymyted, personally to appeare before your good lordshippe in Her Majesties highnes courte of Chauncerie, then and there to answere the premisses; and further to stande to and abyde suche order and direction therein as to your good lordshippe shall seeme best to stand with righte, equytie and good conscyence, and your saide oratours shall daylie praye to God for the prosperous healthe of your good lordshippe with increase of honour longe to contynewe.

4. *Answer of John Lambert.*[1]

Juratus coram me, Thomam Legge, 24 Novembris, 1597. — The answeare of John Lamberte, defendante, to the byll of complainte of John Shakespeare and Mary His wief, complainantes. — The said defendante, savinge to himselfe both nowe, and att all tymes hereafter, all advantage of excepcion to the uncertentie and insufficiencie of the said complainantes byll, and also savinge to this defendante such advantage as by the order of this honorable courte he shall be adjudged to have, for that the like byll, in effecte conteyninge the self-same matter, hath byne heretofore exhibited into this honorable courte againste this defendante, whereunto the defendante hath made a full and directe answeare, wherein the said complainante hath not proceeded to hearinge; for a seconde full and directe answeare unto the said complainantes byll sayeth that true yt is, as this defendante verylie thinkethe, that the said complainantes were, or one of them was, lawfully seized in theire or one of theire demeasne, as of fee, of and in one mesuage and one yearde and fower acres of lande with thappurtenaunces, lyeinge and beinge in Wilmecott, in the parishe of Aston Cawntloe, in the countie of Warwicke, and that they or one of them soe beinge thereof seized, the said complainante, John Shakspeere, by indenture beringe date uppon or about the fowertenth daye of November, in the twenteth yeare of the raigne of our Sovereigne Lady the Queenes Majestie that now ys, for and in consideracion of the summe of fortie powndes of lawful Englishe monney unto the said complainante paide by Edmunde Lamberte, this defendantes father in the said byll named, did geve, graunte, bargaine and sell the said mesuage, and one yearde and fower acres of lande with thap-

[1] Outlines, ii. 15.

purtenaunces, unto the said Edmunde Lamberte, and his heires and assignes, to have and to holde the said messauge, one yearde and fower acres of land, with thappurtenaunces, unto the saide Edmunde Lamberte, his heires and assignes, for ever; in which indenture there is a condicional provisoe conteyned that, if the said complainante did paye unto the said Edmunde Lamberte the summe of fortie powndes uppon the feast daie of St. Michell tharchangell which shoulde be in the yeare of our Lorde God one thousande fyve hundred and eighte, att the dwellinge howse of the said Edmund Lamberte, in Barton-on-the-Heath in the said countie of Warwick, that then the said graunte, bargaine, and sale, and all the covenauntes, grauntes and agreements therin conteyned, shulde cease and be voyde, as by the said indenture, wherunto this defendante for his better certentie doth referre himselfe, maye appeare; and afterwardes, the saide complainante John Shakspeere, by his Deede Pole and Liverie theruppon made, did infeoffe the said Edmunde Lamberte of the saide premisses, to have and to holde unto him the said Edmunde Lamberte and his heires for ever; after all which, in the terme of Ester, in the one and twenteth yeare of the Queenes Majesties raigne that nowe ys, the said complainantes in due forme of lawe did levye a fyne of the said mesuage and yearde lande, and other the premisses before the Queenes Majesties justices of the comon plees att Westminster, unto the saide Edmunde Lamberte, and his heires, sur conuzance de droyt, as that which the said Edmunde had of the gifte of the said John Shakspeere, as by the said pole deede, and the chirographe of the said fine, whereunto this defendante for his better certaintie referreth himselfe, yt doth and may appeare; and this defendante further sayeth that the said complainante did not tender or paye the said summe of fortie powndes unto the said Edmunde Lamberte, this defendantes father, uppon the said feaste daye. which was in the yeare of our Lord God one thowsande fyve hundred and eightie, accordinge to the said provisoe in the said indenture expressed. By reason whereof this defendantes said father was lawfully and absolutly seized of the said premisses in his demeasne as of fee, and, aboute eleven yeares laste paste thereof, dyed seized; by and after whose decease the said messuage and premisses with thappurtaunces descended and came, as of righte the same oughte to descende and come, unto this defendante, as sonne and nexte heire of the said Edmunde; by vertue whereof this defendante was and yet is of the said messuage, yearde, lande and premisses, lawfully seized in his demeasne as of fee, which this defendante hopeth he oughte both by lawe and equite to enjoye, accordinge to his lawful righte and tytle therin; and this defendante further sayeth that the said messuage, yearde lande and other the said premisses, or the most parte thereof, have ever, sythence the purches therof by this defendantes father, byne in lease by the demise of the said complainante; and the lease thereof beinge nowe somewhat nere expyred, whereby a greater value is to be yearly raised thereby, they, the said complainantes, doe now trowble, and moleste this defendante by unjuste sutes in lawe, thinkinge therby, as yt should seme, to wringe from him this defendante some further recompence for the said premisses then they have already received; without that, that yt was agreed that the said Edmunde Lamberte shoulde have and enjoye the said premisses in anie other manner and forme, to the knowledge of this defendante, then this defendante hath in his said answeare heretofore expressed; and without that, that anie deedes or evidences concernynge the premisses that of righte belonge to the said complainantes are come to the handes and possession of this defendante, as in the said byll is untruly supposed; and without that, that anie other matter, cause or thinge in the said complainantes byll conteined, materiall or effectuall in the law, to be answeared unto, towchinge or concernyinge him, this defendante, and hereinbefore not answeared unto; confessed and avoyded, traversed or denied, is true, to this defendantes knowledge or remembrance, in such manner and forme as in the said byll the same is sette down and declared. All which matters this defendante is reddy to averre and prove, as this honorable courte shall awarde, and praythe to be dismissed therhence with his reasonable costes and charges in this wrongfull sute by him unjustly susteyned.

5. *Replication.*[1]

The replicacion of John Shakespere and Mary his wiefe, plentiffes, to the answeare of John Lamberte, defendante. — The said complainantes, for replicacion to the answere of the said defendante, saie that theire bill of complaynt ys certayne and sufficient in the lawe to be answered; which said bill, and matters therein contayned, these complainantes will avowe, verefie, and justifie to be true and sufficient in the lawe to be answered unto, in such sorte, manner and forme as the same be sett forthe and declared in the said bill; and further they saie that thanswere of the said defendante is untrue and insufficient in lawe to be replied unto, for many apparent causes in the same appearinge, thadvantage whereof these complainantes praie may be to theym now and at all tymes saved, then and not ells; for further replicacion to the said answere they saie that, acordinge to the condicion or proviso mencioned in the said indenture of bargaine and sale of the premisses mencioned in the said bill of complaynt, he this complaynant, John Shakspere, did come to the dwellinge-house of the said Edmunde Lamberte, in Barton-uppon-the Heathe, uppon the feaste daie of St. Michaell tharche angell, which was in the yeare of our Lorde God one thousand fyve hundred and eightie, and then and there tendered to paie unto him the said Edmunde Lamberte the said fortie poundes, which he was to paie for the redemp-

[1] Outlines, ii. 16.

cion of the said premisses; which somme the said Edmunde did refuse to receyve, sayinge that he owed him other money, and unless that he, the said John, would paie him altogether, as well the said fortie poundes as the other money, which he owed him over and above, he would not receave the said fortie poundes, and imediatlie after he, the said Edmunde dyed, and by reason thereof, he the said defendant, entered into the said premisses, and wrongfullie kepeth and detayneth the said premisses from him the said complaynant; without that, any other matter or thinge, materiall or effectuall, for these complaynantes to replie unto, and not herein sufficientlie confessed and avoyded, denyed and traversed, ys true; all which matters and thinges thes complaynantes are redie to averr and prove, as this honourable court will awarde, and pray as before in theire said bill they have praied. — *In dorso, Ter. Michael. Annis 40 et 41.*

6. *Orders of Court.*[1]

I. July the 5th, 1598. — *Quinto die Julij.* John Shackspere and Mary, hiswief, plaintiffes, John Lamberte, defendant. A commission ys awarded to examyne witnesses on bothe partes, directed to Richard Lane, John Combes, Thomas Underhill and Fraunces Woodward, gentlemen iij. or ij. of them, returnable *octavis Michaelis*, by assente of the attorneys, Powle and Hubbard, and the plaintieffes to geve xiiij. daies warninge.

II. July 10th, 1598. — *Lune, decimo die Julii.* John Shackspere and Marye, his wief, plaintiffes; John Lamberte, defendante. — A commission ys awarded to examyne witnesses on bothe partes, directed to Richard Lanne, John Combes, Thomas Underhill and Frances Woodward, gentlemen, or two of them, returnable *octavis Michaelis*, by the assent of the attorneys, Powle and Hubbard, and the plaintiffes to give xiiij. days warninge.

[1] Outlines, ii. 204.

III. May the 18th, 1599.—*xviij° die Maij.* John Shakespeare, plaintiff; John Lambard, defendant. Forasmuch as this Court was this presente day ynformed by Mr. Overbury, beinge of the defendantes councell, that the plaintiff did fyrst exhibyte a bill unto this Court against the defendant, as well by his owne name as in the name of his wyef, to be relyved towchinge a mortgage of certene landes lyinge in the county of Warr, made to the defendantes father, whose heyre the defendant is, and afterwards exhibyted a bill in his owne name only concerninge such matter in substaunce as the former bill doth;[1] and althoughe the plaintiff hath taken owt two severall commisyones upon the later bill, yet he hath not examyned any wytnesses thereupon. It is therefore ordered that, yf Mr. D. Hunt, one of the Masters of this Court, shall, upon consideracion of the said bills, fynde and report that bothe the said billes doe in substaunce conteyne one matter, then the defendant ys to be dismissed from one of the said billes, with such costes as the said Mr. D. Hunt shall tax and asseasse; and the plaintiff ys to procede to the hearinge thereof withe effect, and the defendant shal be at lyberty to chaunge his commissyones, yf he will, and the plaintiffes attorney is to be warned hereof. (There is a duplicate entry of this Order, the only variation worthy of notice being the words another bill instead of a bill in 1. 8.)

IV. June the 27th, 1599.—*xxvij° die Junij.* John Shackspere and Margaret, his wief, plaintiffes; John Lamberte, defendante.—A commission ys awarded to examine witnesses on bothe partes, directed to Richard Lane, John Combes, William Berry and John Wanre, gentlemen, iij. or ij. of them, returnable *octavis Michaelis*, by assente of the attorneyss, Powle and Hubard, and the plaintiffes to

[1] The evident mistake in the preamble to this order (a mere *ex parte* suggestion of counsel), that the joint bill of John Shakespeare and Wife was prior in time to the individual bill of John Shakespeare, will be found commented on *ante*, pp. 135, 6.

geve xiiij. daies warninge. (In the contemporary index to the Orders, under Trin. Term. 41 Eliz., there is the entry, — Shackspeere contra Lambert, 896, — but the end of the volume which did contain that leaf is unfortunately missing. The lost note was most probably a duplicate of the Order here given.)

V. October the 23rd, 1599. *Martis, xxiij°. die Octobris.* John Shakespere and Mary, his wief, plaintiffes; John Lamberte, defendant. — Yf the defendant shewe no cawse for stay of publicacion by this day sevenight, then publicacion ys graunted. — (There is a duplicate of this entry in which the surname of the plaintiffs appears in the form of Shakesbere.)

NOTE.

The date of filing the bill (*ante*, p. 161) has been accepted upon the authority of Halliwell-Phillips. It will be noticed that the jurat to the answer bears the same date, Nov. 24, 1597. This may mean one of two things. It may mean that the author has carelessly transferred the date from the jurat to the bill. This is unlikely, in view of the painstaking accuracy habitual to this writer, especially with regard to his dates. The other supposition is that in order to avoid the delay, and particularly the expense, of a subpœna to Warwickshire, the county of John Lambert's residence, and to secure a voluntary appearance, the draft of the bill, before being filed, was submitted to the inspection of his London solicitor, so that both papers might be filed on the same day.

It will be remembered that a previous suit had been instituted and was still pending in the same court, between the same John Shakespeare and the same defendant. The anomalous character of the procedure is commented on, *ante*, p. 136.

APPENDIX C

SHAKESPEARE AS PARTY TO THE LAMBERT COMPROMISE

INDICATIONS AS TO THE NATURE OF HIS INTEREST, INFERRIBLE FROM THE PECULIAR STRUCTURE OF THE "DOUBLE FINE" LEVIED TO ASSURE THE GIBBS LEASE

WHETHER the tenure of Mary Arden Shakespeare in her paternal inheritance of Asbies was that of an estate in fee simple, as heretofore assumed, or of an entailed estate, as hereinafter indicated, is a question in itself of not the slightest importance. It is only worth consideration incidentally, and so far as it may tend to shed light upon an authentic and rare event in her son's biography. That authentic incident is the recorded fact that in 1587 he became personally a party to a proposed compromise of the Lambert litigation.

A question that has never been settled, that has really not been at all considered, is as to the nature of the interest he had in the subject of controversy. If his mother's title was in fee simple, as has been generally supposed, then her eldest son had no interest, that is, no legal interest, during her life, upon the principle *nemo est hæres viventis*. In that case, the only possible explanation for his presence on the scene is the one suggested in the text, namely, the apprehension that he might upon his mother's death file a bill in chancery to impeach the transaction as an undue advantage taken by a mortgagee of a necessitous debtor, by the purchase of an equity of redemption for an inadequate price.[1]

If, on the other hand, his mother's title was that of an

[1] *Ante*, p. 126.

entailed estate, it is at once obvious that, as eldest son and heir in tail, no effective settlement of the controversy could be made without his participation.

The difficulty here is the entire absence of direct documentary evidence. The only instrument we have deriving title is her father's will, and that purports (in terms not artificial) to devise an absolute estate.[1]

There is no other original document extant which throws light upon the question of title, until we come to the *Gibbs lease*. There is only the early conjecture of Halliwell-Phillips of a lost marriage settlement.[2]

When we come to examine the lease in question, or rather the fine levied in the court of common pleas to assure the lease, which is all that is left of the transaction, we are impressed by its apparent circuity and intricacy. Halliwell-Phillips observes that its terms are "peculiar." From our point of view they certainly are as crooked as a ram's horn. Besides John Shakespeare and wife, lessors, and George Gibbs, lessee, two other parties are introduced into the arrangement, "Thomas Webb" and "Humphrey Hooper." These last are made plaintiffs in the fictitious suit, and John Shakespeare and wife and George Gibbs are made defendants. The successive steps in the process are as follows: —

1. The Shakespeares and Gibbs are made to acknowledge the title of *Webb*, and quitclaim to him and Hooper and to the heirs of Webb. 2. The Shakespeares warrant to Webb and Hooper and Webb's heirs. 3. Webb and Hooper lease to Gibbs for twenty-one years at an annual rent of the moiety of one quarter of wheat and the moiety of one quarter of barley, with the usual clause of distraint for rent in arrear. 4. Webb and Hooper grant the reversion and rent back to John and Mary Shakespeare and the heirs of Mary.

[1] Outlines, ii. 53. See Co. Litt. 9 a.

[2] Outlines, second edition, 59, 60.

Such, upon analysis, is found to be the substance of a cloud of law-Latin verbiage which darkens rather more than one of Halliwell-Phillips's ample pages.[1] The circuity of it is mysterious, and the complexity of it is a wonder. Whatever may have been the interests of "Webb" and "Hooper" or their relations to the parties, they were evidently used as men of straw, first to take title, and then to transfer it. The substantial parties were the Shakespeares, the lessors, on the one side, and Gibbs, the lessee, on the other. The result is to leave Gibbs in possession as lessee at a nominal rent (in all about eight bushels of mixed grain), with the Shakespeares as his landlords.

As to the circuity and indirectness of the process, which struck Halliwell-Phillips as "peculiar," it is to be remembered that the structure of the instrument is not to be criticised from the modern standpoint. The "*fine*" as a method of conveyance has been so long happily obsolete, that it is difficult for us to realize how thoroughly artificial and fantastic a device it was. In its original, it was founded upon an actual *bona fide* suit at law for the possession of land; and the title thus acquired was found to be so effectual that fictitious actions were afterwards countenanced by the courts to reach the same satisfactory result.[2] A law writer of Shakespeare's time, after showing the great antiquity of fines, continues: "And at this day, fines be of great force, puissance and worthiness, for being levied and ingrossed with proclamations, they are finall ends, and sufficiently bar, conclude and discharge forever as well parties as privies, as estrangers to the same" not claiming in due time.[3]

"A fine is so called because it puts an *end*, not only to the suit thus commenced, but also to all other suits and

[1] Outlines, ii. 202, 203.
[2] 2 Bl. Com. 349.
[3] 2 West, Symboleography, F. & C. fol. 1.

controversies concerning the same matter."[1] Specifically, their utility was threefold: to extinguish dormant titles, bar or destroy estates-tail, and pass the interests of married women.

"Such are the three chief effects, by reason of which, fines, no longer used as recorded agreements for conclusion of actual suits, have been changed into and are still retained as *feigned* proceedings ; and being thus accommodated to answer purposes to which ordinary conveyances cannot be applied, it is no wonder that they should not only be considered as a species of conveyance, but also be deemed a principal guard to the titles to real property, and as such to be ranked amongst the most valuable of the common assurances of the realm."[2]

The accumulated subtlety of successive generations of lawyers and judges had made the learning of fines satisfactorily abstruse and delightfully intricate. There are tricks in all trades, and a matter so solemn and conclusive as the "levy of a fine" was so arranged as to invariably require expert and expensive professional assistance. The same law writer already referred to holds out terrible threats to those who venture upon this sacred ground without watching, fasting, and prayer. "There should be no false Latin, no rasing, no interlining, — therefore the writ should be examined twice or thrice for errors."[3] With a grim play upon the word, the successive steps required to consummate the process were each attended by the payment of a "*fine*" in the well-known modern sense. Thus the "primer fine" to the king was one tenth the annual value of the land, and the "*post* fine" was three twentieths the annual value.[4] In order to secure publicity equivalent to livery of seisin, the fine (in the technical sense) was to be repeatedly proclaimed in court, and a note of its contents set up in public places.[5]

[1] 2 Bl. Com. 349. [2] Hargrave's note to Co. Litt. 121 a.
[3] 2 West, Symbol. ib. fol. 9. [4] 2 Bl. Com. 350.
[5] Ib. The notoriety of transfer thus supposed to be obtained was, in fact, a very poor substitute for a system of public recording

Professional ingenuity had profitably and pleasantly subdivided fines into four distinct classes, each with its appropriate hard name in law French. A more simple division was that into "single" or "double" fines. As the Gibbs lease was an instance of the "*double fine*," it will be necessary to explain this distinction, which happens not to be at all difficult, barring a single term of art which must first be defined.

The "cognizor" or "conusor" was the party who made "cognizance" or acknowledgment of the feigned preëxisting title of the "cognizee" or "conusee." Viewing the fine simply as a conveyance, the conusor was the grantor, and the other the grantee. Thus, in the Gibbs lease, the Shakespeares and Gibbs posed as conusors, and Webb and Hooper as conusees. This acknowledgment of title in Webb and Hooper was one of the approved fictions, and there was nothing at all "peculiar" in the introduction of these outside parties into the conventional mechanism.

Now, a "*single fine*" is described as one in which nothing is rendered back by the conusees, or any of them, to the conusors, or any of them. A "*double fine*" is one which renders back something out of the land, or the land itself, to all the conusors, or to some of them.[1]

In the Gibbs lease, as already shown, the Shakespeares and Gibbs, as conusors, in effect grant the land to Webb and Hooper, as conusees. Then Webb and Hooper turn around and lease to Gibbs for twenty-one years, and finally strip themselves of what is left, by granting the rent and reversion to the Shakespeares. The practical effect of this "double fine" is that Webb and Hooper come out just as they went in — with nothing. These strangers being eliminated, there are left, on the one side, the Shakespeares as lessors, or assignees of lessors, and Gibbs as lessee.

of deeds which had, with local exceptions, been kept out of England through the dislike of the landed aristocracy to its "inquisitorial" character. (Phelps's Jurid. Eq. 242.)

[1] 2 West, Symbol. ib. fol. 6.

This "double fine" corresponds with the fourth class in the technical subdivision referred to, called the fine *sur done*, being a combination of the fine *sur cognizance* and the fine *sur concessit.*[1]

The question as to the necessity for the introduction of the two outside parties is a far-reaching one, inasmuch as it involves another question, and that is, *whether the title to the Asbies estate was in fee simple or fee tail.* And this latter question involves still another, and that is, the necessity for the *participation of* WILLIAM SHAKESPEARE in the attempted compromise of the mortgage difficulty with Lambert in September, 1587.

First in order, it is necessary to explain that there appear to have been two modes of effecting *a lease for years* by fine; one, when the lessor and lessee were the only parties to the transaction; and the other, when a third party was introduced, having no actual interest. By the first and simple method, an effectual lease was created between the parties, *but not so as to bind issue in tail of the lessor.* The tenant for years might at any time *lose his term by the death of the landlord.* The only reason assigned for this is the technical one, that the issue in tail "taketh by the fine, but giveth nothing thereby." The other method was deemed necessary when the estate was entailed, and the object was to bind the issue. The process is thus described: "*The tenant in tail and the lessee to knowledge the tenements to be the right of an estranger, and the cognizee to grant and render the tenements to the lessee for certain years reserving a rent, etc., and then grant the reversion to the tenant in tail.*"[2]

Here we have the Gibbs lease almost exactly. The only variance is that in the latter there were two "estrangers" brought in. But again we read from the contemporary of

[1] 2 Bl. Com. 353.

[2] 2 West, Symbol. ib. fol. 10, 11; Shep. Touch. 16; Brown on Fines, 37, 47, 149.

Shakespeare: "*Fine levied to divers cognizees, the right shall be limited to one of them only, and the estate limited to his heirs only whose right it is knowledged to be.*"[1] Here, at last, we find the Gibbs lease on all fours. The Shakespeares and Gibbs are made to "knowledge" the title of Webb alone, and the grant and warranty is to him and Hooper and the *heirs of Webb.* Like everything else connected with the operation, this particular feature was purely conventional, depending upon artificial reasoning from collusive and fictitious data.

The significance of the feature (the introduction of Webb and Hooper) is that it indicates the nature of Mrs. Shakespeare's title to Asbies as an *estate tail.* We have a copy of her father's will, but it throws no light upon the inquiry. The devise is in these words: "I give and bequethe to my youngste dowghter Marye all my land in Willmecote cawlide Asbyes, and the crop apone the grounde sowne and tyllide as hitt is."[2] There is nothing else, so far as I am aware, that bears upon this question, except a single circumstance. That circumstance brings into the dusty atmosphere of all this legal pedantry no less a personage than the great WILLIAM SHAKESPEARE himself.

At the age of twenty-three he was a party to the negotiation with John Lambert, which resulted in the agreement of 26th of September, 1587, for the attempted settlement of the mortgage difficulty. By this agreement, John Lambert was to retain the Asbies estate (subject of course to the Gibbs lease) upon paying John Shakespeare twenty pounds in addition to the forty pounds advanced by Edmund Lambert, his father. It was further agreed that John Lambert was to have his title assured by John Shakespeare and his wife, and that *their son*, WILLIAM SHAKESPEARE, *should unite in the conveyance.* Upon the theory that Asbies was an entailed estate, the necessity for making the eldest son and heir apparent a party to the compromise is at once satisfactorily accounted for.

[1] 2 West, Symbol. ib. fol. 10. [2] Outlines, ii. 53.

Thus, these two independent circumstances, the introduction of Webb and Hooper into the fine levied to consummate the Gibbs lease, and the introduction of WILLIAM SHAKESPEARE into the Lambert mortgage settlement, both point to the character of the title which Mrs. Shakespeare held at that time, and indicate that the tenure of Asbies was not a fee simple, but an estate-tail.

And thus the original conjecture of Halliwell-Phillips of a lost "*marriage settlement*" is found to be justified, although he finally abandoned it, with his usual candor, when not successful in finding any supporting proof. If to his sure-footed sagacity there had been added the technical acquirements of the craft, he might have found the evidence required to sustain his shrewd conjecture in the conventional structure of the "*double fine*" levied to assure the lease for a term of years from SHAKESPEARE'S parents to George Gibbs.

The record evidence of the participation of WILLIAM SHAKESPEARE in the attempted compromise of his father's suit is to be found in the declaration filed in the court of queen's bench in 1589, in the case of John Shakespeare *v.* John Lambert; an action of assumpsit to recover damages for breach of contract. The declaration[1] sets forth the mortgage from John and Mary Shakespeare to Edmund Lambert — the entry of Edmund Lambert thereunder — his dying seized — the descent to his son and heir, the defendant — and then goes on to state the contract with John Lambert in the following terms: —

"Dictusque Johannes Lamberte dubitans statum et interesse sua de et in tenementis predictis cum pertinentiis esse vacua et noticiam habens quod predictus Johannes Shackespere eum implacitare vellet et intendisset pro premissis *in consideracione* quod predictus Johannes Shackespere adtunc imposterum non implacitaret dictum Johannem Lamberte pro mesuagio predicto et ceteris premissis cum pertinentiis et quod dictus Johannes

[1] *Ante*, p. 158.

Shackespere et Maria uxor ejus simulcum WILLIELMO SHACKESPERE filio suo cum inde requisiti essent — assurarent mesuagium predictum et cetera premissa cum pertinentiis prefato Johanni Lamberte et deliberarent omnia scripta et evidencias premissa predicta concernentia predictus Johannes Lamberte vicesimo sexto die Septembris anno regni dicte domine regine vicesimo-nono apud Stratforde-super-Avon in comitatu predicto in consideracione inde super se assumpsit et prefato Johanni Shackspere adtunc et ibidem fideliter promisit quod ipse idem Johannes Lamberte viginti libras legalis monete Anglie prefato Johanni Shackspere modo et forma sequentibus videlicet" etc., etc.

The twenty pounds were to be paid by instalments at a place and at times specified in the *narratio*, which claims that the plaintiff performed his part of the contract, — had not brought suit to recover the mortgaged premises, — and brings in WILLIAM SHAKESPEARE again in these words: —

"Quod ipse idem Johannes Shackspere et Maria uxor ejus simulcum WILLIELMO SHACKSPERE filio suo semper hactenus parati fuerunt tam ad assurandum premissa predicta quam ad deliberandum eidem Johanni Lamberte omnia scripta et evidencias eadem premissa concernentia" etc., etc.

The declaration concludes by charging a breach of the contract, by the defendant's failure to pay the plaintiff his twenty pounds, and claims damages to the extent of thirty pounds.[1]

In the latest,[2] and by far the best of the biographies, there is a disappointing reference to this transaction, which is dismissed with the dry and skeptical observation: "But the deed does not indicate that Shakespeare personally assisted at the transaction." [3]

[1] Outlines, ii. 11, 12, where it is stated that "this document contains the only positive notices of the great dramatist between the years 1585 and 1592 which have yet been discovered." (For translation, see Appendix B.)

[2] This was written before the appearance of Mr. Mabie's admirable work.

[3] Lee's Life of Shakespeare, 26.

Passing as too trivial for criticism the verbal slip which makes a "deed" out of a declaration in assumpsit, it may, with deference, be submitted, that the implied doubt is negatived by the usual course of business and by all the probabilities of the situation. Nothing is more unlikely than that a business transaction of so much importance to the family, to the success of which the active concurrence of SHAKESPEARE was an indispensable factor, as involving a personal interest of his own, should have been conceived and carried to the point of a contract without his knowledge, consent, and coöperation. Immediately upon the breach of this contract began the long litigation in the courts of Westminster Hall, which, as previously stated, is agreed by all the authorities to have been backed by WILLIAM SHAKESPEARE from first to last, to the full extent of his means.

If not already made entirely clear, it should be distinctly understood that the introduction of the two "estrangers" into the artificial mechanism of the "double fine" was a contrivance which appears to have been applicable only in the case of assuring "*leases for term of years.*"[1] Hence the marked difference in structure between the "double fine" in question and the "single fine" to assure the Lambert mortgage.[2]

A formidable objection to the theory above presented may appear, at first sight, in certain title references contained in documents connected with the chancery suit or suits of Shakespeare *v.* Lambert.[3] It is true that those title references are appropriate rather to an estate in fee simple than to an entailed estate. But, in the absence of the originals, these vague, second-hand references cannot be taken as conclusive. The surprising carelessness and clumsiness in the drafting of the bill of complaint, appar-

[1] 2 West, Symbol. ib. fol. 10, 11.

[2] See Appendix B. [3] Appendix B.

ent upon the least critical attention, are pointed out in detail in the text.[1] It is shown that the document is throughout a slipshod piece of work, bristling with reckless allegations demonstrably erroneous, and in material points flatly inconsistent with the replication. And more surprising still, it is shown that a palpable mistake in a very simple and obvious matter of fact is actually embalmed in the preamble to an order of court.[2]

Even the more correctly drawn answer of John Lambert appears upon examination to be singularly inaccurate in the only title reference we are enabled to verify. The fine, levied in the court of common pleas to assure the Lambert mortgage, was, of course, the fundamental muniment, the corner-stone, of the Lambert title.[3] The proceeding was indispensable, first, to pass the title of the married woman, *Shakespeare's* mother, and, secondly, if her title was that of an entailed estate, to dock the entail, so far as the mortgage was concerned. Accordingly, we find her properly made a party to the proceeding, and her name aptly introduced into the operative words of the fine, which are, in the original: —

> "*Quod predicti Johannes et Maria recognoverunt predicta tenementa, . . . esse jus ipsius Edmundi, ut illa que idem Edmundus habet de dono predictorum Johannis et Marie.*"

This fine is the only document connected with the mortgage transaction which has come down to us, the indenture and deed poll having been lost. When solicitor Hubard, who appears to have represented the defendant in the chancery suit or suits, came to draw Lambert's answer to the Shakespeares' bill, it would naturally be supposed that he would be very careful in citing the operative words of the fine, his main reliance. If he did make a mistake in citing them, it would at least not be expected that the mistake would be to the disadvantage of his own client.

[1] Chapter xvii.
[2] Order of 15 May, 1599. Appendix B.
[3] See fine translated, Appendix B.

In this instance it was the unexpected which happened. In Lambert's answer we are amazed to find this all important muniment of title, in its operative part, thus cited: "*unto the said Edmunde Lamberte, and his heirs, sur conuzance de droyt, as that which the said Edmunde had of the gifte of the said John Shakespeare.*"

Mary Shakespeare, the real owner, the indispensable party, the party on whose account the fine was especially necessary, is thus negligently omitted from the recital of the instrument, a mistake which might have been disastrous but for the presence of the record itself. And this, let it be remembered, is the only title reference in the whole case whose accuracy we are able to test by comparison with an original record.

It is thus apparent that very little reliance can be placed upon references to title, in either bill or answer.[1] Such references, indeed, have little significance when it is remembered that they were in no wise material to the controversy, the exact nature of Mary Shakespeare's original title to the mortgaged estate not being an issue in the case. These title references, unsupported by exhibits, immaterial, and coming from a source of proved inaccuracy, are not to be considered of sufficient weight to overcome the indications pointed out from the structure of the double fine levied to assure the Gibbs lease. Those indications are, as already seen, that WILLIAM SHAKESPEARE, as heir-in-tail, had an actual legal interest in the Asbies estate (whether in virtue of a lost marriage settlement, as once suggested by Halliwell-Phillips, or otherwise), which accounts for his being brought in, as a necessary party, to the attempted compromise, in 1587, of the Lambert mortgage controversy.

During an obscure and silent interval of seven years (1585–1592), this is absolutely the only incident in the dramatist's biography of which we have the slightest au-

[1] In the declaration there is no reference to the original title of Mary Shakespeare, before the fine which docked the entail.

thentic evidence. For that reason, the investigation has a unique interest, and also because it involves the consideration of a once famous legal process with which he had numerous occasions, besides the one in question, to become practically acquainted, and which furnished a favorite contribution to his much exploited stock of legal terms and calembours.

"Why may not that be the skull of a lawyer? Where be his quiddits now, his quillets, his cases, his tenures, and his tricks? Why does he suffer this rude knave now to knock him about the sconce with a dirty shovel, and will not tell him of his action of battery? Humph! This fellow might be in 's time a great buyer of land, with his statutes, his recognizances, his fines, his double vouchers, his recoveries. Is this the fine of his fines, and the recovery of his recoveries, to have his fine pate full of fine dirt?"[1]

[1] *Hamlet*, Act V. scene 1.

APPENDIX D

COKE AND SIR TOBY BELCH

THE connection between Coke's famous vituperation of Ralegh ("For I *thou* thee, thou traitor") and Sir Toby's "martial" directions to Aguecheek for his challenge to Viola ("If thou *thou'st* him some thrice") was suggested [1] upon the authority of Lord Campbell. Upon the same authority was suggested the connection between Sir Toby's sarcastic skit and Coke's charge against players as vagrants to the Norwich grand jury, while Coke was recorder of that city.[2]

By some critics objection has been taken to this very natural view of Campbell and others as an anachronism. According to some authorities *Twelfth Night* was composed in 1600 or 1601. According to Halliwell-Phillips, "*Twelfth Night*, the perfection of English comedy, and the most fascinating drama in the language, was produced in the season of 1601–2, most probably on January the fifth, that is, on Twelfth Night, 1602." [3]

Ralegh's trial did not take place until November, 1603.[4] It is of course quite obvious that if the amusing satire of the jovial Sir Toby on the afterwards famous expression "thou," used by Coke as a verb, stood as part of the text in its original form, it could have had no reference to an incident which had not at that time occurred.

1 *Ante*, p. 71.

2 Campbell's Lives of the Chief Justices, ch. vii.; I. 222, 280, citing Boswell's Shakespeare, ii. 442. See, also, annotation to the report of Ralegh's trial in 2 Howell's State Trials, 10.

3 Outlines, i. 200; note 69, ii. 282.

4 2 Howell's State Trials.

These critics forget, however, or fail to appreciate, the very material fact that the comedy was not in print at the time of the trial, nor for many years thereafter. The play was first printed in the folio of 1623.[1]

At the time of the trial and afterwards, the text was wholly subject to the author's revision. It was open to any additions that might be suggested by circumstances as they arose, by any interest or by any motive. The text was in a plastic state. It was in a state to have stamped upon it "the very age and body of the time, his form and pressure." It was in a state which facilitated and invited the insertion of a local hit or gag, whenever furnished by a current notoriety or passing folly.

While the unpublished manuscript of *Twelfth Night* was under the control of the author, in the condition referred to, there occurred the most conspicuous and exciting event that had taken place since the recent accession of James the First. A number of persons, more or less prominent, including Lord Cobham, Lord Grey, and Sir Walter Ralegh, were charged with treason and tried for their lives. The trial took place at Winchester, before an extraordinary tribunal. It resulted, as state trials in those days commonly resulted, in conviction. Three were executed, with all the sickening details of carnage and cruelty characteristic of the age. Three had their heads upon the block when their pardons arrived. Ralegh was committed to the Tower, with the death sentence suspended over his head, and kept there many years before he was brought to the block.

It may well be supposed that the thrilling incidents attending and following this historic state trial furnished the most sensational news of the day. There was no event to compete with it in attracting public attention. No topic was more largely discussed in the inns of court, in the taverns, at the theatres, or on the street.

[1] Dyce's Shakespeare, iii. 310.

All London, at least all of Shakespeare's London, was ringing with the fame of the vile epithets and atrocious insults hurled by Sir Edward Coke, attorney-general, at the head of Sir Walter Ralegh. With emotions as varied as the sympathies of the crowd, there would be alternate indignation and laughter as the words were repeated from mouth to mouth: —

"Thou art a monster; thou hast an English face but a Spanish heart." "The absolutest traitor that ever was." "The notoriest (*sic*) traitor that ever held up his hand." "Thou art the most vile and execrable traitor that ever lived." "Spider of hell."

But the insult most apt to be remembered and frequently quoted was the ludicrous explosion: "Thou viper; for I *thou* thee, thou traitor." [1]

Nothing can be more likely than that the author of *Twelfth Night* would be instantly struck by the exquisite humor of this speech, when made available as a satire upon the pedantic, irascible, and stage-hating attorney-general.

The exact place for its introduction was at hand in the challenge to Viola, dictated to Aguecheek by the gay and festive Sir Toby Belch. And that the gag was there interpolated as an afterthought appears also from internal evidence. Notwithstanding the visible effort to adjust the context to the interjected phrase, the rough joint is easily perceived in the broken connection between "taunt" and "lies."

The whole passage will be quoted as printed,[2] and the reader will be left to judge for himself, without any attempt at argument, whether or not the strong probability at least is that the immediate context as first written stood thus, — "taunt him with the license of ink and as many lies as will lie in thy sheet of paper," etc.; that the passage originally ended with the words, "bed of Ware in England;" and that the words, "set 'em down," originally constituted a

[1] 2 Howell's State Trials, 10. [2] Camb. ed.

distinct and separate command of precisely the same imperative purport, note, and emphasis as the succeeding phrase, "go, about it."

"*Sir Andrew:* Will either of you bear me a challenge to him?

"*Sir Toby:* Go, write it in a martial hand; be curst and brief; it is no matter how witty, so it be eloquent and full of invention: taunt him with the license of ink: if thou *thou'st* him some thrice, it shall not be amiss; and as many lies as will lie in thy sheet of paper, although the sheet were big enough for the bed of Ware in England, set 'em down: go, about it. Let there be gall enough in thy ink, though thou write with a goose-pen, no matter: about it."[1]

[1] *Twelfth Night*, Act III. scene 2.

INDEX

The Riverside Press
Electrotyped and printed by H. O. Houghton & Co.
Cambridge, Mass., U. S. A.

FALSTAFF AND EQUITY

PRESS NOTICES

This book comes as a surprise, a luminous interpretation which the professional searchers have all overlooked. In style graceful, forceful, sparkling, full of wit and humor, and altogether worthy to stand alongside the best that has been written. — *Law Notes.*

Judge Phelps has accomplished the phenomenon of adding something new to the Shakespearean commentaries. Mr. Henry Austin Clapp in his Introduction aptly terms it "of its kind the most curious and surprising candle of illumination that has been newly lighted within several years." — *Boston Journal.*

Curious, and of unusual interest, full of quaint matter, rich in forgotten lore, pithy and pointed. — *Brooklyn Eagle.*

A most charming essay, sparkling with that delicate wit whose "prosperity lies in the ear of him that hears it." A welcome addition to Shakespeareana, and an excellent adjunct to the elementary study of law, being in its way as worthy of commendation as "Ten Thousand a Year." — *N. Y. Commercial Advertiser.*

A treasure trove for the Shakespearean student. An original and scholarly study, and, while of especial interest to students of the evolution of law, is yet written in a style so clear that it is of great interest to laymen. It is a notable contribution to Shakespearean literature. — *The Book Buyer.*

There are much law and learning in the book, and much humor withal, and it is all set forth with great vivacity and piquancy of style. Lawyers and students of Shakespeare will equally enjoy it. — *The Critic.*

It is dry work to anatomize an old and forgotten jest, but the author has thrown in so many interesting details of life at the time, and added so much solid learning to his discussion, that the reader's interest never flags. — *The Independent.*

Lawyers will read Professor Phelps's witty and acute comments with rare delight, and those who know nothing of Coke upon Littleton will find the style so modern and idiomatic, that they will enjoy the work scarcely less. — *The Watchman,* Boston.

An important addition to special Shakespeare studies. The book is interesting from cover to cover. — *The Outlook.*

The discussion by Judge Phelps is clear and masterful. His argument is original. — *The Dial.*

A fascinating little volume, admirably written, and by no means intended for the Shakespearean specialist. — *Evening Post,* Chicago.

A deeply interesting and illuminating treatise. — *Globe Democrat*, St. Louis.

A notable addition to Shakespearean literature. One which the lawyer and student of Shakespeare will alike enjoy. — *The Literary World*, Boston.

A discovery both curious and interesting. — *Tribune*, Cambridge.

We can assure every student of the bard of Avon that exquisite pleasure awaits him in its perusal. — *Albany Law Journal.*

One of the best of the commentaries. —*American Lawyer.*

A searching and brilliant exposition of a difficult passage, in a charming and interesting style. — *Baltimore Sun.*

Really delightful reading, even though it attempts that very daring feat, the explanation of a joke. — *Springfield Republican.*

Through his legal revelations there runs a quaint humor, the charm of the volume. — *Town and Country*, New York.

Students of the immortal bard will find in the book a large amount of interesting reading. — *Law Times*, London.

Will be found of especial interest to all English-speaking judges, lawyers, and law students, as well as to all interested in Shakespeare's personal biography. — *Review of Reviews.*

An ingenious and learned monograph. — *The Nation.*

A treat to the lawyer and the lover of Shakespeare; to the lucky mortal who is a student both of the law and the great dramatist, it is nothing short of a feast. The author deserves high rank as a discoverer in the field of literature. — *The Green Bag*, Boston.

The documents were printed long ago by Halliwell-Phillips, but have remained insufficiently understood for want of such legal criticism as Judge Phelps now brings to them. — Sir FREDERICK POLLOCK, in *The Law Quarterly Review*, London.

The book is really of much greater value than its name and purpose indicate, The history of the great judicial war is so entertainingly told that the reader is likely to forget ere he turns fifty pages that it is all for the sake of explaining a joke. — *The Forum*, Carlisle, Pa.

The matter of this delightful book is of an exceptional character, and will interest students of English law and history everywhere, though its prime appeal is to Shakespeareans. The volume will take high rank for its originality and acumen, as well as for the charm of its sparkling and effective style. — *Boston Advertiser.*